The Community of the Faithful

Jesus as a Personification of Servant Israel

ARSH KHAIRA

Foreword by Steven Muir

WIPF & STOCK · Eugene, Oregon

THE COMMUNITY OF THE FAITHFUL
Jesus as a Personification of Servant Israel

Wipf & Stock
An Imprint of Wipf and Stock Publishers
199 W. 8th Ave., Suite 3
Eugene, OR 97401

www.wipfandstock.com

PAPERBACK ISBN: 978-1-6667-0829-5
HARDCOVER ISBN: 978-1-6667-0830-1
EBOOK ISBN: 978-1-6667-0831-8

NOVEMBER 29, 2021

Contents

Foreword

AT ONE LEVEL, THIS BOOK presents an original and insightful examination of two key motifs in early Christian Christology: the suffering servant of Isaiah and the son of man of Daniel. Traditionally in Christian theology, the texts describing these figures have been viewed as prophecies concerning the messianic role of Jesus of Nazareth: to suffer and to be glorified. Khaira nuances that understanding by considering the individual person of Jesus in relation to his community, the people of Israel. Khaira argues persuasively that we gain a richer understanding of the activities and intention of Jesus by considering how he deliberately fulfilled in his own life (a microcosm) the destiny of his people (the macrocosm), shaped by the above motifs. The effect of taking such a destiny and focusing it into a single person is powerful.

The above point leads to the second level of this book, and one of its true values. The questions raised here, and the answers given, are more than a historical or even theological analysis. They show what it means when one person chooses to be a fully committed and responsible member of a group. To what extent do we today, as individuals, feel any relation to the groups which define our identity? To what extent do we contribute to the success not only of ourselves but to the group as a whole? To what extent are we prepared to take responsibility and to make personal sacrifices for the good of the group? I write these words in the fall of 2021, when the COVID-19 pandemic has profoundly brought these timeless questions into focus.

While I hope that this book has an enduring appeal, I also see it as a timely comment on society today. I urge the readers to read it at both levels. You will find it engaging, persuasive, and moving.

Dr. Steven Muir
Professor of Religious Studies
Concordia University of Edmonton

Preface

TRADITIONAL CHRISTIAN THEOLOGICAL INTERPRETATIONS view
the "suffering servant" of Isaiah as an individual, messianic figure
with an inherent eschatological purpose. This same view attests
that this figure was fulfilled by the person of Jesus. The "son of
man" in the revelation of Daniel is viewed in a similar way, and
again, this prophecy is understood in traditional Christian interpretations as having been represented conclusively by Jesus.

My proposed hypothesis takes into consideration an alternative view of the suffering servant and the son of man, in that both
were used by the exilic prophets to describe the wounded nation
of Israel. With regard to the first: bound to exile, anguished and
compelled to defeat in Babylon, and cast away from their covenant
promise. With the latter: in their future restored state as the "light
to the nations" (Isa 42:6; 49:6; 60:3) and as "shepherds of peace"
(Ps 23), completely connected to God in a relationship of perfect
obedience.

The second part of my interpretation is to show that Jesus understood what the exilic prophets meant, he understood what the
nation of Israel had to go through to be restored—namely, a death
and resurrection experience—and he understood himself as the
actualization, or personification, of the ideal nation under God.
The nation of Israel was then manifest by himself as a singular
personification of God's people. Jesus' role, then, was to undergo
a literal death-and-resurrection experience in order to restore the

nation to their covenant promise as a righteous community of the faithful.

The last part of my interpretation takes the Gospel of Luke and the promise of the kingdom of God, which I propose follows a realized eschatological scenario in which the kingdom represents the full and final extension of God's plan for Israel. The aim of my proposed interpretation is to enrich our traditional understanding with a new perceptual lens by which to recognize the person of Jesus, his mission, and his purpose.

Acknowledgements

I gratefully acknowledge the guidance of Dr. Steven Muir for his inspiration and support in the completion of this task. I am also thankful to Dr. Adrian Leske for motivating the vision behind this project and to Dr. Gerald Krispin for his encouragement.

I would like to dedicate this book to the memory of the late Dr. Richard Kraemer, whose friendship and kindness were a major inspiration for my pursuit of biblical scholarship.

Opening Remarks

THE JEWISH PROPHETS OFTEN spoke of their nation-community in a distinctive way—they described Israel as a person. They spoke of the requirements necessary for Israel to accomplish in order to reenter into a relationship with God, as their previous relationship with God had been broken. The prophets suggested that one of these requirements, or features, necessary for their nation to undergo was the experience of a death and resurrection. This death and resurrection sort of experience was understood as having happened twice before, once during Israel's bondage in Egypt (death) and subsequent restoration to their land (resurrection); and the second time in Israel's exile and bondage in Babylon (death), with the resurrection experience being their restoration by the Persians. The prophets often spoke of these experiences as being undertaken by a single person—whom Isaiah called the suffering servant, and whom Daniel called the son of man—when in actuality, these experiences were undertaken by their entire community. The individualized portraiture of the prophets gives vitality and poignancy to their predictions.

Jesus, as a son of Israel, understood what the prophets meant. He knew what the prophets had written about Israel, about their past, and about their future—he was aware of the prophetic tradition. The singular person that Israel used to describe themselves, although symbolically, came to be personified in Jesus. He came to be the lone individual who stood for an entire nation, not only symbolically, but *literally*, as the embodiment of true Israel, as

1

everything that Israel was meant to be according to God's plan. With this, and with his awareness of the prophetic tradition, Jesus lived in a relationship to God that was exactly what the relationship between Israel and God was meant to be. Not only was Jesus a son of Israel, but he was from the line of David. Jesus not only accepted his role as being that of true Israel, but he understood the requirements necessary for Israel to reenter into a relationship of obedience to God, the same requirements as spoken of by the prophets—a death and resurrection experience that not only Israel but *all* the nations would come to witness. In his own ministry and sacrifice, Jesus would actualize this death and resurrection experience in the purest way; he would suffer and die on behalf of his people.

In this way, the life, death, and resurrection of Jesus became the fulfillment of the prophecies of the Jewish prophets, in particular the revelations of Isaiah and Daniel. Israel now, through faith in one of their own people—in a special way, their own son— could reenter into their covenant relationship with God. Every requirement necessary for them as a nation to complete as spoken of by the prophets had been completed by Jesus. As Jesus stood in an ideal relationship with God, now the people of Israel, through their own death and resurrection, stood in a fulfilled relationship of obedience and promise to God. The necessary element of this new relationship became faith in their absolution, by what their scapegoat—their son—had achieved. The death and resurrection experience of Israel, spoken of by the prophets, was in this way actualized by the person of Jesus. This in essence represented the commencement of the new covenant as explicated in Jer 31: 31–34.[1]

The new covenant now becomes a relationship between faithful Israel and God, in which their ultimate vocation, as written in the original covenant relationship, becomes manifest in a growing universal reality, shown in the imminence of the kingdom of God—a universal certainty which follows a "realizing" eschatological scenario. In this way, Israel's calling to act as a light to

---

1. Note that I will further explicate these ideas in the following research.

the nations finally and conclusively reaches its crescendo, as now Israel is joined by a universal community, bound together by the new covenant relationship which began in the works and miracles of servant Israel, Jesus. This is what I mean by Israel's death and resurrection experience: their concept of themselves as an ethnically and geographically bounded, exclusive 'people of God' had died; and it was reborn in a new definition as a community of the faithful joined by brothers in faith who were universal in composition and location: the house of Israel.

Through the death and resurrection of Jesus, now not only are the faithful of Israel vindicated, but in the completion of the necessary experiences spoken of by the prophets—which would see the salvation of Israel and the return of their role to shepherd the nations to faith—the rest of the world can enter into the new covenant relationship with them as brothers in faith. This in essence sees the fulfillment of the promise to the house of David of everlasting dominion, as spoken of by the prophet Daniel in Dan 7:14: "His dominion is an everlasting dominion that will not pass away, and his kingdom is one that will never be destroyed."[2] We may compare this with Luke 1:33: "He will be great and will be called the Son of the Most High. The Lord God will give him the throne of his father David, and he will reign over Jacob's descendants forever; his kingdom will never end." In essence, in the death experience of the Servant, the remnant of Israel which emerges as the faithful—as written in Isa 10:22, which we may compare with Rom 9:27—become the ones from whom the covenant promise is passed on to the nations, who enter into a relationship of discipleship and brotherhood as the house of Israel. Israel then returns in some ways to the original covenant promise of everlasting dominion, with a kingdom that has now extended to include the faithful of the gentile world who have joined them as brothers in faith.

Many prophets suggested that only a remnant of Israel would be saved from their burdens and doom: "Though your people, O

2. This book will make use of the NKJV translations of the text unless otherwise noted.

Israel, be like the sand by the sea, only *a remnant* will return" (Is 10:22, emphasis mine). We see this concept also in Joel 2:32:

> And everyone who calls on the name of the Lord will be saved; for on Mount Zion and in Jerusalem there will be deliverance, as the Lord has said, among *the survivors* whom the Lord calls. (emphasis mine)

Jesus' followers came to understand that this remnant of Israel would place their faith in their absolution by their Messiah Jesus and become the righteous of Israel, the faithful few who were vindicated. They now stood in a perfect relationship to God, a relationship which had been actualized by Jesus (true Israel). Now, the covenant promise originally made to *nation* Israel would spread to others throughout the world by the works of discipleship in proclaiming God's covenant relationship completed through *person* Israel (Jesus). The new Israel was then joined by believers from the gentile world as brothers in faith who felt that the story of Jesus and his vicarious sacrifice connected with their own lives and situations. They, too, became members of the house of Israel, and in this way, the community of the faithful grew and continues to grow today. Herein is the promise of the kingdom of God—not solely a future event or place but rather the historical and ongoing, true reality of Israel in a relationship of perfect obedience to God. The kingdom began with the life and sacrifice of Jesus, and now is in a continual state of realization, and will continue to grow until its full fruition in the future when the kingdom of Israel comes to serve the entirety of humanity. This community of faithful believers, then, assumes the symbolic physical presence of Jesus the Messiah in the new age. This is a significant point. Just as the person Jesus once personified and fulfilled the role of 'people of God', now the community of the faithful represents and continues the work started by the person Jesus. Jesus' return from heaven has begun in the ongoing presence of his essence—through his word and gospel, and physically through his people, who heal, teach, and proclaim on his behalf.

It is this perspective which I intend to demonstrate in this book.

Introduction

TRADITIONAL CHRISTIAN THEOLOGICAL INTERPRETATIONS hold to the view that the Jewish prophets of the Old Testament were granted revelations of a future messianic figure. From a Jewish perspective, in their own historical context the prophets spoke in a descriptive and predictive way about a future figure and often described him as being the one through whom a restoration of the relationship between Israel and God would be fulfilled. The traditional Christian view is that the prophets spoke of this messianic figure as the one who would come to absolve the people of the world of their sufferings—namely, estrangement from God and the will of God. In this way, the figure spoken of by the prophets in various contexts is understood by Christians to have been fulfilled by the person of Jesus.

I will demonstrate that while this interpretation is perfectly valid, there is another way to read and understand these scriptures with regard to the messianic figure spoken of by the Jewish prophets which supplements and deepens this view. In this interpretation, we can understand that the Jewish prophets were given insight by God into the nature of human community. Often, they would particularize this communal ideology with regard to their own nation of Israel, but at a more abstract level, we can see that they also spoke in a revelatory way about a society in its ideal state (regardless of ethnic or geographic boundaries). What they are describing is a society that would exist in full accordance with the will of God. The Jewish prophets would at times portray this community as a singular person—in other words, they personify the collective and idealized community as an individual. I estimate that here, the prophets were speaking in a symbolic and idealized way.

The early followers of Jesus understood him to have embodied the collective identity of the idealized community of which the prophets spoke. The personification of this community was found to have been fulfilled by the person of Jesus, a *person* of God standing in a symbolic relationship to the *people* of God. The reality of human existence in divine accordance with God was fulfilled by the person of Jesus; thus, the commencement of the collective destiny of the people of God similarly began through him. Followers of Jesus have faith that he has brought into the reality of human existence the collective destiny of the people of God, and that by having faith in the one who brought about the new reality, they, too, participate in the promise spoken of by the Jewish prophets of a community in its ideal state. This ideal community, which includes the remnant of faithful Israel as well as gentile brothers in faith, will herein be referred to as the house of Israel or the righteous of Israel—those who, through the sufferings endured by the personification of the restored community, Jesus—came to be vindicated.

I suggest that the above-mentioned interpretation, which speaks of the microcosm of Jesus standing in relation to the macrocosm of human society, allows us to better understand his purpose with respect to what the Jewish prophets were saying in their own historical contexts. This view does not negate the traditional Christian reading; rather, it both gives it greater depth and, as I will demonstrate, is more consistent with the worldviews and understanding of the Jewish prophets and Jesus' first followers. Among such people, there was a high degree of group solidarity and collective identity, and the model I will present does justice to the ancient worldviews of the prophets and their people, and also resonates with the hopes and aspirations of spiritual people today.

This book will examine this collective personification idea by looking first at Isa 53 and the figure of the suffering servant. I will describe how this figure is traditionally interpreted in a broad Christian view as a messianic redeemer prophesied by Isaiah and fulfilled by the person of Jesus. I will apply my proposed interpretation to show that the suffering servant was actually used by Isaiah to describe a righteous community of the elect of God, personified as a singular person. This passage describes the necessity of a death and resurrection experience by the servant, so that Israel may reenter into a restored relationship with God, but that in a futurist, eschatological sense, this community now includes all of those who had been vindicated through the works of the servant Jesus, including the remnant of faithful Israel and gentile brothers in faith, together as the house of Israel.

To show what the ideal relationship between the people and God would look like, the prophet Isaiah used the figure of a servant, a personification of the people of God. We see that Jesus stood in relationship to God in a very direct way, and he embodied what the relationship between the people and God was to be. He actualized the prophetic portrait of Isaiah—Jesus was that servant. In this way, many Christians accept his death and resurrection as the act by which their community would enter into a complete relationship of obedience to God. The prophets contextualized their view of the relationship of humanity to God by considering the relationship of their people, Israel, to the Creator, and it was Jesus, standing in perfect obedience to YHWH, that personified what Israel was meant to be.

I will then describe how the texts of Dan 7:13–14 describe a similar situation. Daniel uses the term "son of man" to explore the same idea as Isaiah. This section will look at how my proposed interpretation of the Jewish prophets as having spoken of a community of believers in a state of perfect obedience to the will of God can be further evidenced from Daniel's description of the son of man. The term has traditionally been interpreted as describing the intercession of a universal messiah figure with a saving eschatological function. I will show how these traditional interpretations do not fully exhaust the meanings of the text; and that my view, which shows that the term was used to describe an ideal community in a restored relationship of obedience to God, is closer to the views of the Jewish prophets and allows us to better understand the historical calling of Jesus. This will be done by showing that Jesus personified certain characteristics and ideals which were similar to the son of man figure as described in the Old Testament. The prophets were speaking of an ideal community in obedience to God through the perspective lens of their own community, Israel. Jesus, then, understanding the prophetic context, came to stand as a faithful representation, or idealization, of that perfect community. In essence, he was the personification of the perfect community, standing in a relationship of obedience to the will of God, as spoken of by the prophets. In this way, Jesus became true Israel, and the agent through which the faithful remnant of the house of Jacob was vindicated. The promise to Israel, then, lends itself to a more universal reading in which the gentile followers of Jesus join the house of Israel as brothers in faith, perpetuating the message of this new universal kingdom of Israel through the teaching and proclaiming of God's promise to the world.

The insights from Daniel and Isaiah will be further developed in later chapters by examining the passion narrative of Matthew and the way that Jesus' self-identification as the son of man shows his awareness of the prophetic tradition. Jesus stands in relationship to God the way the son of man (Israel) is meant to according to the Jewish prophets. Israel is to be fully obedient to YHWH and to have a relationship with him that is exactly the same as the relationship Jesus had to God. In the first chapter dealing with Matthew, I will describe how the son of man and suffering servant figures spoken of by the prophets were fulfilled by the person of Jesus. While on the surface this does not seem to be a deviation from the traditional Christian theological perspective, the difference in my interpretation can be found in the way Jesus fulfills the messianic hopes of the Jewish people. I will show in this section how Matthew describes to his audience that Jesus is God's agent for the people of Israel, the one through whom the covenant promise to the house of Jacob can come to full fruition. However, now, the faithful remnant of Israel are joined by the nations of the world as brothers in faith, therein fulfilling the promise first made to Israel of an everlasting and universal kingdom. Matthew writes in a very clear and distinct way; he clearly engages his Jewish audience in the traditions of the prophets and shows them how Jesus lives up to all of the qualities and characteristics that the Jewish people are meant to in their traditional covenant relationship with God. In this way, when Matthew shows Jesus as self-identifying as the son of man, he shows the Messiah's awareness of the prophetic tradition. In this section, I will further attempt to demonstrate that Jesus embodies the characteristics of servant Israel, and personifies the collective community of God in his person.

In the second chapter dealing with Matthew, I will explore the realized and futurist elements of the first gospel writer's eschatology. I will demonstrate how the relationship of humanity to God was restored by the person of Jesus, thus creating a community of believers who stand in direct obedience to God, and collectively embody what true Israel was to be. I will do this by looking into issues of Matthean authorship and audience, and into the original message of the gospel writer. In this section, I will also examine and create a segue into the social eschatology of Jesus. I will do this by presenting a framework that conceptualizes the works and miracles of Jesus as agents of social change in the greater fabric of society. Because this, in my interpretation, represents the commencement of the kingdom of God on earth, I will then transition into the imminent reality of the kingdom of God as the subject of my final chapter.

My final chapter will look at the gospel of Luke as the best source to summarize my arguments with regard to the greater community of the faithful as an extension of God's plan for Israel. This in essence represents the commencement of the kingdom of God on earth, or, as the next section of my analysis indicates, the kingdom of God as a realized eschatological event in which the relationship of the people to God is reestablished in the death and resurrection of the servant of Israel. I will demonstrate how the original promise to Israel came to full fruition in the death and resurrection of Jesus. Herein, the promise to the house of Jacob, as explicated in the new covenant relationship of Jeremiah, commenced in the history of the new community of the people of God. This new community—the righteous of Israel, or the restored house of Israel—then come to represent the physical presence of Jesus in an age of restoration which will come to full fruition at some point in the future. As this promise of a universal kingdom comes closer to realization, the physical presence of Jesus grows accordingly through his body, the community of the faithful, who heal, teach, and proclaim on his behalf.

Messianic Expectation in the Old Testament

The Suffering Servant in Isaiah

AUTHOR, AUDIENCE, DATE, AND PURPOSE

To HELP US UNDERSTAND ideas surrounding authorship of this text, I turn first and primarily to Friedman and Ginsberg—who show us that it is widely held in contemporary scholarship that the Book of Isaiah was written in two parts by two distinct authors. The first of these authors is Isaiah himself (the son of Amoz who was the brother of Amaziah, king of Judah), who wrote chapters 1–39 and whose prophetic career spans the years 740–700 BCE in Jerusalem. He was preceded slightly by Hosea and Amos, both of whom preached in the Northern Kingdom.[1] The beginning of his prophetic career is mentioned in Isa 6:1: "In the year that King Uzziah died, I saw the Lord, high and exalted, seated on a throne." We may estimate that this event happened in 740 BCE, as this event coincided with "the onset of a highly critical period in the fortunes of both the kingdoms of Israel and Judah,"[2] and the events of this period are the background to Isaiah's prophecies in chapters 1–39.

Friedman and Ginsberg further show us how chapters 40–66 of the Book of Isaiah contain the revelations of an unknown prophet during the Babylonian exile. This notion of the book is

1. Friedman and Ginsberg, "Isaiah," 57–75.
2. Friedman and Ginsberg, "Isaiah," 59.

known as Deutero-, or "Second," Isaiah. The key event outlined in this section is the conquest of Babylon by Cyrus the Persian and his kingdom, which is mentioned in Isa 45 and 47 and can be dated to the year 539 BCE.[3] This section carries on toward the restoration of Israel, and this section of the book will be my primary source in the following research. The purpose of the Book of Isaiah, according to Friedman and Ginsberg, is ultimately to declare two key messages. Firstly, the book affirms not only an emphasis on the holiness of God but also a rejection of the reliance on human schemes and wisdom to continue the destiny of Israel. The book teaches of a total reliance on God to accomplish the fortune of Israel and that through faith in Jerusalem as the unfaltering city of God, it would become the future site of a "universal acceptance of the God of Israel by the nations."[4] Secondly, the book further describes the "delineation of the messianic king under whose reign final justice and peace will be inaugurated" and the doctrine that only a "remnant of Israel shall emerge out of the doom to be visited upon it."[5]

ISAIAH 53 AND THE SUFFERING SERVANT

I have proposed an alternative interpretation into the message of the Jewish prophets Isaiah and Daniel. While it is traditionally accepted that the prophets were given revelations of a future messianic figure, described in passages such as Isa 53 and Dan 7, I propose that these verses were written to provide insight into the nature of an idealized community in a restored relationship with God. In essence, these scriptures describe the way the relationship between the people and God can be renewed, and also function as descriptions of the way this bond will exist in the future. In the context of Isaiah and Daniel, the prophets describe the future existence of an idealized community that exists in a restored

3. Friedman and Ginsberg, "Isaiah," 59.
4. Friedman and Ginsberg, "Isaiah," 59.
5. Friedman and Ginsberg, "Isaiah," 59.

relationship with God through the lens of their own community Israel. They understand that Israel must undergo a death and resurrection experience in order to be made righteous once again before God, and in the following section, I will describe how Isaiah expounds this idea in detail.

Isaiah uses the history of Israel and their future expectations to describe in essence what the true community of God will look like at some point in the future. As Israel's relationship to God at this point is broken, Isaiah describes that the nation will need to go through a death and resurrection experience now in order to reestablish their relationship to God as his chosen people. Isaiah describes that in the future, the righteous of Israel will be made up of the community of believers who have participated in the death and resurrection experience of the servant, their self-identification, and will see their everlasting dominion and glory.

I recognize two perspectives on the identification of the suffering servant as presented in the Servant Songs of Isaiah. The first is the traditional Christian theological interpretation, which proposes that the suffering servant figure prophetically points to Jesus, and that his death and resurrection occurred on behalf of all humanity and for the absolution of sin. As Otto Betz has stated, it was "the will of his heavenly Father that the Son must suffer and save his people from their sins,"[6] as in Matt 1:21: "And she will bring forth a Son, and you shall call his name Jesus, for He will save His people from their sins." There is no denying the centrality of this interpretation within Christianity, and its importance in the doctrine of justification.

However, I propose that a second interpretation is not only possible but warranted when we consider the original context of the Old Testament prophetic literature itself and the purpose for which these texts were initially written. In line with McKenzie, I suggest that here, the suffering servant represents not "an individual person but the personification of a group,"[7] the collective faithful of Israel who had to undergo the ordeal of the exile, a kind

6. Betz, "Jesus and Isaiah 53," 70.
7. McKenzie, Second Isaiah, xliii.

of death and resurrection experience, in order to be vindicated and made righteous in the eyes of God due to their transgressions against him. McKenzie helps us understand that the oldest forms of interpretation of these passages see "in the Servant a personification of the people of Israel,"[8] and this is most clear in that "Israel is called the Servant of Yahweh several times in the text of Second Isaiah."[9] The passages in Isa 40–66 detail the fate of servant Israel over and against the nations who are persecuting them and have caused them to become exiled in the first place: "Sit in silence, and go into darkness, O daughter of the Chaldeans; for you shall no longer be called the lady of kingdoms. I was angry with my people; I have profaned my inheritance, and given them into your hand" (Isa 47:5–6).

During the intertestamental period and later, Jewish prophetic literature often was interpreted in order to have the prophecies comment on current or future events. Melugin shows us that we may consider whether "Isaiah 53 shaped the self-consciousness and the understanding of the personal calling of the historical Jesus,"[10] or if that connection originated "in the early church after the time of Jesus."[11] Melugin helps us see that this process of re-reading the old prophetic texts, which lasted from the mid-fourth century BCE during the reign of Alexander the Great up until the coming of Jesus and later into the history of early Christianity, is what led the Jerusalem church to proclaim "Christ's death on the cross as the fulfillment of Isaiah 52:13–53:12"[12]: "For He made Him who knew no sin to be sin for us, that we might become the righteousness of God in Him" (2 Cor 5:21). Again, the centrality of this concept in Christian theology is undeniable.

8. McKenzie, *Second Isaiah*, xliii.

9. McKenzie, *Second Isaiah*, xliii.

10. Melugin, "On Reading Isaiah 53 as Christian Scripture," in Bellinger and Farmer, *Suffering Servant*, 55.

11. Melugin, "On Reading Isaiah 53 as Christian Scripture," in Bellinger and Farmer, *Suffering Servant*, 55.

12. Melugin, "On Reading Isaiah 53 as Christian Scripture," in Bellinger and Farmer, *Suffering Servant*, 55.

I propose, however, that the above does not exhaust the interpretations of the text. I suggest that we may investigate whether the role of Jesus was not simply to recontextualize the prophetic material to his current situation and his own purpose but to reiterate and personify certain principles and ideals. I suggest that as a teacher to the Jews of his day, Jesus sought to reinvoke, or bring to current experience, the message of the prophets in their historical context as addressed to the role and plight of "servant Israel"— whom Jesus personified in his words and actions. Clements makes this clear by showing that in this way, the "sufferings endured by an individual are effective in bringing healing and forgiveness to a larger group,"[13] and this is what "lends the portrait of the Servant much of its uniqueness."[14] Jesus became "servant Israel" and went through a death and resurrection experience in order to make the faithful of Israel righteous before God.

Jesus spoke of the interaction between servant Israel and the nations in a new way. This differed from the typical way in which Israel had previously seen this relationship—namely, that the other nations of the world represented the wicked and they themselves represented the righteous. We see that view in the following quote: "To him whom man despises, to him whom the nation abhors, to the Servant of rulers: 'Kings shall see and arise, princes also shall worship, because the Lord who is faithful, the Holy One of Israel; and He has chosen you'" (Isa 49:7). Rather, I estimate that Jesus spoke of the brotherhood of humanity, wherein the covenant promise to Israel had been extended to all the nations of the world: "Go therefore and make disciples of all nations, baptizing them in the name of the Father and of the Son and of the Holy Spirit" (Matt 28:19).

I propose that when Isaiah speaks of the "suffering servant," we may view that he is speaking about the servant Israel as a faithful nation or collective, rather than an individual messianic figure.

13. R. E. Clements, "Isaiah 53 and the Restoration of Israel," in Bellinger and Farmer, *Suffering Servant*, 40.

14. R. E. Clements, "Isaiah 53 and the Restoration of Israel," in Bellinger and Farmer, *Suffering Servant*, 40.

McKenzie explicates this view in that the "Servant is not historic Israel, neither the whole of Israel or its faithful core, but Israel idealized, an Israel aware of its mission and dedicated to it,"[15] and in this way "the Servant so conceived can only exist in the future."[16] By this, the death and resurrection of Jesus can be seen as an act at once culminating the nation's past history and commencing a definitive new phase in the final purpose of faithful Israel. This principle, when read into the prophecy of Isaiah, creates a template, likely adopted by Jesus himself, in which he lived an ideal life and voluntarily underwent death on behalf of his people as the personification of servant Israel. The Jewish concept understood that there must be a death and resurrection experience in order to be made righteous in the eyes of God—and this process was actualized in the person of Jesus.

I do not mean to suggest that Isa 53 does not have deep messianic implications. But prior to reading Isaiah simply as a "Christian" prophecy, I propose that it is sound exegetical principle to seek to understand it in its own historical context and by what the prophet was telling his audience, the people of Israel. Clements clarifies that to solely interpret the texts in "historical and literary isolation from their present setting in Isaiah 40–55"[17] is often stated in most traditional theological interpretations. While this more traditional Christian interpretation will be presented later, at this point I will highlight the purpose of Isa 53 and the suffering servant in light of the history and events described in Isa 40–66. It should be kept in mind that the messianic implications of these texts are still necessarily there and implied; however, they are most fully understood through a process which involves first a reading of the book of Isaiah in its own historical climate, and second a reading of the prophecy in a Christian light.

Clements further shows us that the primary problem in the interpretation of the figure of the servant lies in the "highly

15. McKenzie, *Second Isaiah*, xliv.

16. McKenzie, *Second Isaiah*, xliv.

17. R. E. Clements, "Isaiah 53 and the Restoration of Israel," in Bellinger and Farmer, *Suffering Servant*, 39.

individual portrayal of the servant set out in the final song (Isa 52:13–53:12)," and the significance of this individual figure in light of the use of the first person "we" in the fourth song. Furthermore, the servant is addressed as "Israel" in Isa 49:6, and this supports the collective interpretation of the figure in the servant passages.[18] Herbert shows us it is evident that the most "sensitive Jewish thinkers have seen the Servant as Israel, so often persecuted through the centuries after the exile,"[19] and while Christian interpreters have understood the prophet, "especially in Isaiah 53, as pointing to Christ," the most important question still lies in asking, "What did the prophet mean in his own day as he spoke to the people before him?"[20] In the traditional Christian approach, this servant figure is seen as a messianic redeemer prophesied of in the text, fulfilled by Jesus through his works and ministry. However, in light of the context in which the prophetic material was written, it is clearly evident that the writer is referring to the faithful of Israel. Herbert wants us to consider that frequently in the Old Testament, "a social group is spoken of in individual terms,"[21] as in Isaiah 1:5–6, where the author describes the nation as a severely wounded individual. It is likely, then, that in the servant poems, the original audience would naturally equate the servant with Israel. Herbert shows how the prophet speaks to his people on behalf of their failures and shows them that they have not been abandoned by God but have been called to a rebirth, to take up what was "from the beginning their ancient role."[22]

It is important to note that the messianic themes we see in the context of Isa 40–66 are in some ways different from the messianism we encounter earlier in First Isaiah, particularly 9:1–6: "For to us a child is born, to us a son is given, and the government will be on his shoulders" (NIV). Another theme akin to this sort of

18. R. E. Clements, "Isaiah 53 and the Restoration of Israel," in Bellinger and Farmer, 40–41.

19. Herbert, *Prophet Isaiah*, 11.

20. Herbert, *Prophet Isaiah*, 11.

21. Herbert, *Prophet Isaiah*, 12.

22. Herbert, *Prophet Isaiah*, 13.

messianism (of great use in early Christocentric doctrines) is the allusion to the branch from the root of Jesse in First Isaiah, as in 11:1–9: "A shoot will come up from the stump of Jesse; from his roots a branch will bear fruit. The spirit of the Lord will rest on him" (NIV). Herein we see a different kind of messianism, a type which is closer to the traditional Christian understandings that I have discussed earlier. Namely, that when read christologically, the New Testament acts as a *telos* of the Old Testament, and Jesus fulfills the prophetic expectations of the Jewish prophets. I do not disagree with this mainstay of Christian doctrine; rather, I hope to enrich that particular understanding with my interpretation of the messianic implications of Second Isaiah in particular. I estimate that the messiah of Isaiah 40–66—the suffering servant in particular—is a personification of the collective identity of Israel.

Muilenburg helps us to note that while the various poems of 40–66 portray a difference in mood and tonality from earlier Isaiah, ultimately they are bound by the common thread of "the promise of the return, the glorification of Yahweh, the redemption of Israel, and the servant of the Lord."[23] Muilenburg also shows that with particular regard to the redemption of Israel, 40–66 explicates most vividly that the nation's God is about to appear, mainly as a "conqueror and victor over Israel's enemies, as a king to usher in his kingdom."[24] Consider for a moment the role of the writer of Second Isaiah as a poet. The writing of 40–66 is so steeped in vivid symbolisms that on the one hand, it may be interpreted as a literal form of prophecy; yet on the other hand, chapter 53 is a vibrant poetic portrait of the writer's people Israel, whom he visualizes as a singular person, a suffering servant of God. Muilenburg expresses this idea in that the writer is "both poet and prophet, and both in a pre-eminent degree."[25] He states that the author is "so much the poet, so much a master in the art of poetic composition, that one can never be unaware of his literary genius."[26] Why, then, would

23. Muilenburg, "Book of Isaiah," 385.
24. Muilenburg, "Book of Isaiah," 385.
25. Muilenburg, "Book of Isaiah," 386.
26. Muilenburg, "Book of Isaiah," 386.

it be difficult for his readers to embrace his literary techniques as seen in his extended questions—some of triadic form—which only explain how the writer of Second Isaiah "apprehends a central characteristic of Hebraic mentality"?[27]

Muilenburg notes that the poem of the coming salvation in Isa 51:1–16 declares most lucidly the "comforting of Zion by the repeated assurance that the time of her deliverance is at hand."[28] Essentially, it is the promise of deliverance and future salvation which permeates all the poems of Deutero-Isaiah. I argue that the servant song of chapter 53 should be taken in the context of the rest of Deutero-Isaiah. When we shape our understanding of the poem of the suffering servant in light of the preceding poems, we can come to wholly understand my proposition of an alternative reading of the song of the suffering servant, in a Christian light.

In this way, the Jewish thinkers of the exile and today are well justified in seeing the role of the servant, especially in Isa 53, as one involving the entire Jewish community, or Israel, who must be vindicated. But there is still room for the traditional Christian interpretation of this passage in the broader context of Isaiah. The role of Jesus as taking the place of the individual in the servant song to redeem the faithful of Israel should be considered, especially in light of reading Isaiah in its own historical context. Janowski shows this through the way that the "we" figures who stand for all of Israel in the Servant Songs eventually come to "see themselves and their guilt represented in the fate of another—the Servant whom they formerly despised."[29] The acceptance of Jesus by the righteous of Israel here becomes the act by which the existence of an idealized community in a restored relationship with God begins. Those who see the person of Jesus as the fulfillment of what servant Israel was to be become a part of the community of the faithful, those who are given the new promise of the covenant. Note that the vicarious taking of guilt by the servant of Israel here

---

27. Muilenburg, "Book of Isaiah," 388.

28. Muilenburg, "Book of Isaiah," 589.

29. Janowski, "He Bore Our Sins," 48.

is an allusion to the figure of the scapegoat on the Day of Atonement, as in Lev 16:20–22:

> Aaron shall lay both his hands on the head of the live goat, confess over it all the iniquities of the children of Israel, and all their transgressions, concerning all their sins, putting them on the head of the goat, and shall send it away into the wilderness.

Betz helps us to support the view that Jesus applied Isaiah's song of the suffering servant to himself, and we can find scriptural evidence pointing to continuity in passages such as Luke 22:37 and, most importantly, in Mark 10:45 and in 14:24: "This is my blood of the new covenant, which is shed for many." We may see this verse in light of the statement "The Son of Man will give his life as a ransom for many," (Isa 53:10). This view is again expressed at the Last Supper in Jesus' statement that his covenant blood is "poured out for many" (Matt 26:28), as is stated also in Isa 53:12: "Because he poured out his soul unto death."[30] But in essence, it is Jesus' role as the servant of the Lord, or suffering servant, which allows him to redeem faithful Israel from their transgressions. The fourth Servant Song is a description of God's new way for Israel after the old way had failed to lead them to their righteous place as servants of God's will and to becoming a witness of salvation to the nations. As Hanson describes, the servant, then, is "God's agent for opening up that new way,"[31] as the "infirmities and diseases . . . have accumulated without relief or cure to the point of dragging the nation to the brink of extinction."[32]

Westermann shows that from Isa 40 onward there is a positive message that God will again deliver his people so that they may begin to live as a nation again. In chapter 52 of Isaiah, Zion is called to "awake" in preparation, and in this the "lamentation

---

30. Otto Betz, "Jesus and Isaiah 53," in Bellinger and Farmer, *Suffering Servant*, 70.

31. Paul D. Hanson, "The World of the Servant of the Lord in Isaiah 40–55," in Bellinger and Farmer, *Suffering Servant*, 17.

32. Paul D. Hanson, "The World of the Servant of the Lord in Isaiah 40-55," in Bellinger and Farmer, *Suffering Servant*, 17.

made by Israel, enslaved and in exile, is finally and conclusively given its quietus."[33] Herein we see the promise of deliverance to Zion—in that the servant shall be lifted up (Isa 52:13) and all the nations shall be astonished at Israel in their resurrection. Referring to Israel in the first person, Isaiah speaks of the righteous of God who have suffered because of the wicked ones who have caused the exile. The righteous of Israel have had to bear the sickness and wounds of those who had transgressed against the Lord, and because of this they have had their grave made "with the transgressors," which refers to the Babylonians and the "rich man" Nebuchadnezzar. By this, the literary interpretation of Isaiah as expressing the plight of servant Israel is again emphasized to supplement the traditional Christian view—such as that expressed by Robert B. Chisholm[34] or Christopher Wright Mitchell[35]—which would read the suffering servant as a prophecy written to expound the suffering experiences of Christ. However, there is an intersection between these two views in that prophetic literature can both have its historical and contextual meaning and be understood in light of Jesus' coming as a Messiah figure.

ANALYSIS OF ISAIAH 52:13–53:12

Herbert is helpful again here, as he shows us that the fourth Servant Poem of Isaiah 52:13–53:12 is seen by Jewish scholars as "portraying the suffering of the Jews down through the centuries,"[36] while Christians from New Testament days onward have "seen this poem above all others as fulfilled in the life, death and resurrection of Jesus, and therefore also of the community of his followers, the Church, in the purpose of God."[37] The poem begins with God's exaltation (52:13–15) and vindication of his servant: "Behold,

---

33. Westermann, *Commentary*, 240.
34. Chisholm, "Christological Fulfillment."
35. Mitchell, *Our Suffering Savior*.
36. Herbert, *Prophet Isaiah*, 108.
37. Herbert, *Prophet Isaiah*, 108.

My Servant shall deal prudently; He shall be exalted and extolled and be very high" (Isa 52:13). Herbert explains how this section represents the "total reversal from humiliation to exaltation of the Servant," where what "the nations and the kings could not see will be revealed in a moment of illumination."[38] Westermann also assists us in building our perceptual lens by showing that verses 13–15 also represent the origin of the servant's work in that he is addressed with the introduction "Behold, My Servant." This is the same introduction to the servant as used in 42:1–4, and this usage is clearly deliberate in that both sections declare the designation of the servant's office by God, which is culminated by God's proclamation in chapter 52 of the "success of his Servant's way and work."[39]

Motyer provides us with important information here as well. We see that 52:13–15 also speaks of the exaltation of the servant which follows the cruel suffering he endures. In verse 13, the prophet commands Israel to watch and "see," the last in a series of commands which follow from 51:1. In all of the exaltations that will be placed upon the servant, the nation is left with questions as to how all such things will take place, to which the final command is to wait and watch—watch the servant and see how he carries out his fortune. The consequence of the servant's way and works brings a threefold exaltation of the servant, who is raised, lifted up, and highly exalted.[40] According to Motyer, this can be linked to the threefold exaltation of Jesus in the resurrection, ascension, and heavenly enthronement.[41]

Herbert shows that in Isa 53:1–2, the following question is made: Can it really be true that the "one so humiliated and despised is the one upon whom God's victorious power rests?"[42] Consider that this is the one to whom the "arm of the Lord" has been revealed (53:1). It is the assertion of Motyer that this symbolism

38. Herbert, *Prophet Isaiah*, 110.
39. Westermann, *Commentary*, 258.
40. Motyer, *Isaiah*, 332.
41. Motyer, *Isaiah*, 332.
42. Herbert, *Prophet Isaiah*, 112.

really alludes to the servant *being* the arm of the Lord, but that he is also *truly* human, as shown in 53:2.[43] For he (the servant) grows before him (the Lord) as a "tender plant," and as a "root out of dry ground" (53:2).[44] This tells us that the servant is not only truly human but that he has a traceable human ancestry.[45] Motyer also asserts that in acknowledging the servant as the arm of the Lord, we can paraphrase Isaiah as asserting that this is actually the Lord himself who has come to act in salvation, as promised in 52:10 ("The Lord has made bare his holy Arm") and that all the nations shall see the salvation of the God of Israel.[46] Motyer clearly likens these properties of the servant as allusions to a Christocentric reading of the person of Jesus, his divinity, and his characteristics. I do not argue against this. However, Motyer's assertions can also be used to supplement my proposed view. It is not the task of this work to engage in a thorough debate on Christology, but rather to supplement and deepen the traditional Christian messianic views of the Servant Songs.

Westermann explains that what follows is a report on the servant's suffering which, on the one hand, "presents the contrast between the Servant's humiliation and his exaltation," but also represents a "confession on the part of those who experienced salvation," as seen in 53:4 ("Surely he has borne our griefs and carried our sorrows") in that the "suffering had been caused by their guilt."[47] Motyer also asserts here that the servant is the agent and the people are the uncomprehending onlookers. But Motyer also mentions that only by revelation could the people really understand the person of the servant, and that his sufferings were in reality theirs. Motyer sees Matt 8:17 as fulfilled in the healing works of Jesus.[48] Herbert shows how in Isa 53:4-6, the "contrasts between the new and old judgments are vividly presented, and

43. Motyer, *Isaiah*, 333.

44. Motyer, *Isaiah*, 334.

45. Motyer, *Isaiah*, 334.

46. Motyer, *Isaiah*, 333-39.

47. Westermann, *Commentary*, 257.

48. Motyer, *Isaiah*, 334.

lead to the confession of sin in verse 6," wherein the "sufferer is not the sinner," in that the "Servant suffered for the sins of others, and by his sufferings brought about a total restoration of health and well-being" ("And by his stripes we are healed" [53:5]). This is "accepted as a revolutionary fact in which God himself is involved."[49]

Westermann explains that in verses 7–9, the picture changes "from sickness to suffering inflicted by others," and the use of the words *born, suffered, died,* and *buried* in response to a human life "results in a structure corresponding to that of the (Apostles') Creed."[50] According to the interpretation of Westermann, this itself would make it "perfectly certain that the Servant song thinks of the Servant as an individual."[51] Herbert shows that ultimately, the "obvious meaning of the language in these verses is that the Servant has unjustly been put to death and buried in a felon's grave."[52] Herbert explains that this condition, followed by the restoration of life in verses 10–12, could mean "reinvigoration," as in Hos 6:2: "After two days he will revive us; On the third day he will raise us up, that we may live in His sight" (Hos 6:2). In this way, "separation from God was death; restoration to fellowship with God was life."[53]

Motyer interprets verses 7–9 as describing first the place of execution (7), then the execution itself (8), and then the burial (9). He shows how it is clear that verses 4–6 have already established that we are to think of the sacrifice of the servant in Levitical terms, in that like a lamb he is led to slaughter but remains silent, in that he has foreknowledge of all things. Motyer's readings are high on Christology, as he further maintains that with regard to the Levitical sacrifices for sin, it is the servant, who is fully human, who actually knows within himself what sin is, as no animal can comprehend this, and "ultimately, only a person can substitute for people."[54] I also argue that Christology, as a central component of

49. Herbert, *Prophet Isaiah*, 112.

50. Westermann, *Commentary*, 264.

51. Westermann, *Commentary*, 264.

52. Herbert, *Prophet Isaiah*, 113.

53. Herbert, *Prophet Isaiah*, 113.

54. Motyer, *Isaiah*, 336.

Christian doctrine, can in essence be supplemented with my view on the nature of the servant and the fulfillment of these prophecies by the person of Jesus.

Westermann explains that verses 10–11 here represent God's turning toward the servant and "his intervention on his behalf," as well as the point where the servant sees salvation.[55] The divine utterance with which the poem ends in verses 11b and 12 is "an oracle attesting the truth of the statement made in their confession by the people whose attitude had changed":[56] "And he bore the sin of many, and made intercession with the transgressors" (Isa 53:12).

Tharekadavil shows that the poem first "speaks about the death and burial of the servant, then about his future life that will see his offspring and the long days of life (vv. 8–10)," in that he "was put to death, and buried with the accompaniments of shame":[57] "For he was cut off from the land of the living" (Isa 53:8). As the poem first speaks about the death and burial of the servant and then about his future life, the first question, according to Tharekadavil, is whether the "text speaks about a real death of the Servant or not."[58] If the servant will prolong his days through his suffering and will divide the spoil with the mighty, one "cannot speak about the actual death of the Servant; therefore the alleged death and burial of the Servant is only metaphorical."[59] Furthermore, the text speaks about multiple deaths, yet a person cannot die more than once. The most notable point, according to Tharekadavil, is that the "metaphor of afterlife was employed by the biblical authors of the exilic and post-exilic period in order to depict the idea of the national restoration of Israel,"[60] as we may confirm by citing Ezek 37:1–14: "Thus says the Lord God to these bones: 'Surely I will cause breath to enter into you, and you shall live" (Ezek 37:5). Tharekadavil shows that here, the reference to the servant as Israel

55. Westermann, *Commentary*, 257.
56. Westermann, *Commentary*, 258.
57. Tharekadavil, *Servant of Yahweh*, 143.
58. Tharekadavil, *Servant of Yahweh*, 143.
59. Tharekadavil, *Servant of Yahweh*, 143.
60. Tharekadavil, *Servant of Yahweh*, 143.

and the death and resurrection experience as metaphorical is an allusion to the idea of the exilic and post-exilic writers, as is shown in Ezekiel in that "if the Servant will submit his soul as an offering, he will see offspring and long days (v. 10)."[61]

Ultimately, in this alternative approach to interpreting the Servant Songs of Isaiah, the purpose of Israel is being redefined throughout these passages. This purpose is twofold: to acknowledge that the God of Israel is the only true God, and to spread this message and promise to the nations of the world.

THE CONVENTIONAL INTERPRETATION

In this method of interpretation, the four Servant Songs of Isaiah and their messianic implications are understood in light of Conzelmann's "salvation history," or *Heilsgeschichte*,[62] which in Christian thought starts after the fall in the Old Testament and continues until humanity is absolved in the vicarious suffering and death of Christ: "Because you have done this, you are cursed more than all cattle, and more than every beast of the field" (Gen 3:14); "Therefore I say to you, every sin and blasphemy will be forgiven men" (Matt 12:31). With this in mind, a brief survey of what salvation history entails will be examined, followed by Isaiah's role in this history through what are said to be his prophecies of a messianic figure found in the four Servant Songs.

It is accepted in this approach that creation is a precursor to salvation. It was, however, the voluntary failure of Adam and Eve in the garden to follow God's command which mingled evil with the human will and led to humanity entering into a disobedient state with God: "Then the eyes of both of them were opened, and

61. Tharekadavil, *Servant of Yahweh*, 144.

62. The concept of *Heilsgeschichte*, or "salvation history," is the work of the German scholar Hans Conzelmann. He contributed to the study of Luke's Gospel by ascertaining that Luke's emphasis actually moved away from the other Gospel's expectations that Jesus would return soon after his ascension to heaven. Rather, Conzelmann believed that Luke's Gospel shifted toward seeing God at work in a history that Christians were to become a part of by being disciples of Christ.

MESSIANIC EXPECTATION IN THE OLD TESTAMENT

they knew that they were naked; and they sewed fig leaves together and made themselves coverings" (Gen 3:7). Where once obedience to God was the dominant force in man's destiny, disobedience now came to replace it as the primary cause of humanity's broken relationship with God. It was the fall in Gen 3 that came to represent the commencement of a life of suffering alienation and estrangement from God's will. At this point, not only was death introduced, but humanity's relationship with God was severed. In the conventional Christian theological understanding, the Old Testament recounts stages in the restoration of humanity's relationship to God, and this begins a narration of God's salvation history. YHWH is portrayed as a saviour God who first acted through the individual salvation of obedient Abraham, from whom the blessing was spread to the nation of Israel and eventually to the world through Jesus: "Now the Lord had said to Abram: 'Get out of your country, from your family and from your father's house, to a land that I will show you. I will make you a great nation; I will bless you and make your name great" (Gen 12:1–2). Without salvation or a restored union with God, humankind was destined to a life of suffering and disobedience. In the conventional interpretation, the Servant Songs of Isaiah represent the critical prophecy or foreshadowing of the definitive act of God's salvation history: the vicarious death of Jesus—"Behold! My Servant whom I have chosen, my beloved in whom My soul is well pleased! I will put my spirit upon Him, and He will declare justice to the Gentiles" (Matt 12:18; cf. Isa 42:1).

With this, the salvation history of humanity comes to a crescendo, marking the commencement of an imminent kingdom of God. This kingdom of an ideal community manifest on earth is marked by an eschatological scenario that is at once realized—as the community has come into existence and will continue to grow unto dominion—but also futurist, in that this kingdom of the elect will come to its full fruition at some point in the future. According to Hans Conzelmann, salvation history is marked by three distinct phases: Israel, Jesus, and the church.[63] Hatina helps us see that in this way, the salvation history of the promise and consequent

63. See Conzelmann, *Theology of St. Luke.*

27

fulfillment of what I would like to call the true covenant community or the righteous of Israel is in essence a movement from "Israel to Jesus to the Pauline mission."[64] And in this way, according to Hatina, to expound one understanding of *Heilsgeschichte*, "Christianity grew out of and was the extension of Judaism."[65] This is in essence Conzelmann's interpretation of salvation history, and this idea of a realized kingdom of God in which the community of the elect has commenced but will come to fruition at some time in the future will be explored in a later section.

A COMPARISON BETWEEN THE TRADITIONAL INTERPRETATION AND THE ALTERNATIVE READING

In the traditional Christian interpretation, within the context of the four Servant Songs in Isaiah, we encounter thematic passages detailing the nature, works, and sufferings of a figure in Old Testament scripture: the servant. It is the characteristic anonymity of the "suffering servant" that facilitates depictions of his nature, which can be understood symbolically and allegorically, based on various historical and relevant contexts.

In the traditional Christian view, the Servant Songs in Isaiah provide a preview of one who would come to bear the sins of many—namely, the person Jesus. Not only are these texts said to allude to the purpose of the Messiah, but they are said to provide a most articulate description of his character. Furthermore, his nature, will, strength, and vocation, as well as the eschatological purpose of his death, are declared prior to his historical fulfillment of this prophecy.

A thematic motif in the traditional theological interpretation of the Servant Songs of Isaiah is the redemption of the sins of all humanity:

Surely He has borne our griefs

64. Hatina, *Biblical Interpretation*, 172.
65. Hatina, *Biblical Interpretation*, 172.

And carried our sorrows yet we esteemed Him stricken,
Smitten by God, and afflicted.
But He was wounded for our transgressions,
He was bruised for our iniquities;
The chastisement for our peace was upon Him,
And by His stripes we are healed.
All we like sheep have gone astray;
We have turned, every one, to his own way;
And the LORD has laid on Him the iniquity of us all. (Isa 53:4–6)

The traditional Christian interpretation of this passage says that it is an allusion to the redemptive act of the suffering and death of Christ—not an explicit allusion to the torment of servant Israel or a personification of their community. Wilken et al. shows us that an example of this traditional understanding can be found in Cyril of Alexandria's commentary on Isaiah, where Cyril notes that Christ "did not suffer on behalf of himself, that was in no way necessary, but on behalf of everything under heaven."[66] The vicarious suffering of Jesus at the cross is, then, the principle allusion of Isaiah in this passage, according to the traditional method.

Assuming the traditional Christian theological interpretation, we see continuity between the Old Testament and passages in the New Testament. For example, in John 1:29 we see the statement that Jesus died so that "he might take away the sin of the world." Also, in Paul's letter to the Romans, he says that since God "did not spare His own Son, but delivered Him up for us all, how shall He not with Him also freely give us all things?" (Rom 8:32). In these passages, it can be seen that maintaining continuity with the Old Testament was a critical issue for the New Testament writers. For the traditional interpreters, the Servant Songs of Isaiah are the sine qua non of christological prophecy in the Old Testament. Mitchell shows us that in the traditional interpretation, Isa 52:13–53:12 "vividly portrays the sufferings of Christ and explicates the

---

66. Wilken et al., "Isaiah," 418.

theology of Christ's vicarious atonement in an exceptionally lucid manner."[67]

One of the theological cornerstones of the traditional Christian understanding of Scripture is the acceptance of christological fulfillment of Old Testament prophecy. We can understand this perspective as it is articulated by Gese, who shows that in this method of interpretation, the New Testament is placed not as a separate series of texts but as the end, or *telos*, of Old Testament theology, one whose teachings logically bring the Old Testament to an end, conclusion, or completion.

A key issue in estimating the primary focus of the passages in Isaiah is whether they are best understood simply as messianic predictions (descriptions of a specific future agent of God), or whether a more nuanced reading is closer to the context and worldview of the author and audience.

To understand the Old Testament as a historical process of development, we may engage the idea that messianism could very well be a post-Isaian concept, perhaps arising in the revelatory context of the New Testament writers. When we compare Matt 3:17 ("This is my Son, the beloved, in whom I was well pleased") to Isa 42:1 ("Behold! My Servant whom I uphold, My Elect One in whom My soul delights!"), we see that the Matthean voice from the heavens as recorded by the New Testament writers has carefully been narrated so as to be in harmony with Isaiah's prophecy. According to the traditional Christian understanding, with the hermeneutical key of reading Old Testament texts christologically intact, traditional interpreters believe they can guarantee the meanings of Isaian prophecy in light of the redemptive work of Jesus.

So, many scholars have defended the traditional Christian interpretation of messianism within the four Servant Songs. However, there is also scholarly discussion as to whether the Servant Songs of Isaiah would more authentically (from a historical-critical perspective) be interpreted within the context of all of Second Isaiah. According to Heskett, the role of the servant in the four

---

67. Mitchell, *Our Suffering Savior*, 15.

songs is different from the role of the servant in other passages
in Second Isaiah—for example, the deviation between the servant
as a collective identity and the servant as an individual.[68] Heskett
shows that it is this dichotomy which further supports the arguments distinguishing the servant as Israel (the collective) on one
hand and Jesus the Saviour (the person) on the other hand.

Christopher North shows us that insofar as Jewish messianic
interpretations are concerned, it is known that the "earliest witness to the messianic interpretation of Isa 53 after the beginning
of the Christian era is the Targum of Jonathan ben Uzziel."[69] North
explains, however, that its "main content must go back to the early
Christian era," as mainstream Jews of the time likely would not
have begun to interpret the servant as a Messiah, since Jesus' followers had already claimed that title for Christ.[70] This Targum is
the first known source which messianically interprets the Servant
Songs. Beyer explains how the second view, however—which suggests that Israel should fulfill Isaiah's description of the suffering
servant—is based on the assumption that the perspective of Isaiah
52:15, which states that the kings of the earth are amazed at the
impact the nation of Israel have on the world, is continued in Isaiah 53:1–12, which "reflects the thoughts of the nations, who saw
Israel as a Suffering Servant of its God."[71]

The traditional theological interpretation proposes that in
Isaiah 52:13–53:12, the prophet predicted the life and work of Jesus
of Nazareth, who was born some seven hundred years later. While
I will argue that the suffering servant should be identified as the
righteous of Israel, both in their nation-state and in their personification by Jesus, it is the act in which the servant suffers on behalf
of his people that I would like to emphasize. The scapegoat figure
was not uncommon in early Judaism, and as mentioned earlier,
this was a common theme that the prophets spoke of throughout
the texts of the Old Testament. The seemingly unjustified suffering

68. Heskett, *Messianism*, 149.

69. North, *Suffering Servant*, 11.

70. North, *Suffering Servant*, 11.

71. Beyer, *Book of Isaiah*, 210.

of the pure sacrifice in the traditional interpretation is understood through the context of Isa 53:7–9:

> He was oppressed and He was afflicted,
> Yet He opened not His mouth;
> He was led as a lamb to the slaughter,
> And as a sheep before its shearers is silent,
> So He opened not His mouth.
> He was taken from prison and from judgment,
> And who will declare His generation?
> For He was cut off from the land of the living;
> For the transgressions of My people He was stricken.
> And they made His grave with the wicked—
> But with the rich at His death,
> Because He had done no violence,
> Nor was any deceit in His mouth.

These verses make it clear that the servant's death was undeserved, as is seen in the last sentence stating that this figure (he/they) had done no violence. It is also shown that the servant's death is voluntary. The servant is led "like a lamb to slaughter," but he does not open his mouth. The servant's voluntary suffering and death is a necessary element of the entire scenario, as it allows us to understand the scope and accomplishment of such an act. In the traditional interpretation of this text, the suffering is thought to predictively portray the vicarious death of Jesus as a willing sacrifice on our behalf. While I agree both that Jesus' death was a willing sacrifice and that it had vicarious efficacy, I estimate that the passage likely is speaking of Israel in the exile and their condition prior to their salvation.

Our alternative reading suggests that with the accepted understanding of the Messiah as one who could activate and restore to Israel the promises made to David after the monarchy had ended, we find fully capable allusions to the Jesus of the New Testament. As an apocalyptic figure, the opposing traditional interpretation suggests his role was not only to redeem humanity for their sins but to act as a cosmic judge upon his return from heaven. It is my view, however, that the eschatological element in the context of these texts points to an idealized community made up of the faithful of Israel, who shall come to represent the true triumph of the servant. Furthermore, the physical presence of Jesus at the second coming will be on behalf of this idealized community, the righteous of Israel—those who have been vindicated on behalf of the sufferings of the servant Jesus.

To further consider the alternative reading and understand the allusions to the future work of the church in a realized kingdom of God—as I will describe in a later section, with insight from the perspective of Leske—consider that in Isa 52:15, the prophet says that the servant will be the one to "sprinkle" many nations and that he will carry out the holy work of God, an allusion to the priestly law and the purification rights of the priesthood. In essence, it becomes the people as a whole, as a living people of the covenant, who will come to carry out the act of "sprinkling" and purifying the many who will be declared righteous. This suplements my view that the servant is a personification of the people of Israel, and later that the house of Israel comes to personify Jesus, as the body of Jesus is the church carrying out the tasks for which they are responsible.[72]

According to Chisholm, in the fourth Servant Song of Isaiah, the nation of Israel "confesses that the one whom they rejected and wrote off as an object of divine wrath is really their savior and destined to be their king."[73] Chisholm also believes that the texts of the fourth Servant Song function to describe "an individual eschatological interpretation . . . which likewise refers to a suffering individual of the dawning end-times" or to an "end-times high priest."[74] Chisholm also shows evidence "that already in the pre-Christian period, traditions about suffering and atoning eschatological messianic figures were available in Palestinian Judaism."[75] I suggest that Chisholm's interpretive method helps us to see how the prophecy of the coming Messiah maintained an element of

72. Leske, *Prophetic Vision*, 54.
73. Chisholm, "Christological Fulfillment," 402.
74. Chisholm, "Christological Fulfillment," 402.
75. Chisholm, "Christological Fulfillment," 402.

realized eschatology which saw fulfillment upon the death of Jesus, ushering in an age in which humanity was absolved but that will be further "realized" in the age of the parousia (according to salvation history).

In the traditional Christian view, as the Word became flesh, Jesus embodies the lyrical revelations of the prophets and encompasses the divine essence of their God. This book holds that along with the traditional interpretation of Isa 53, the alternative reading approach—which argues that Isa 53 is speaking of Israel coming out of the exile with a new understanding of its role to bring many to righteousness—is of great significance in a comprehensive study. In the New Testament, it is Jesus who exemplifies the role that Israel needs to play as the servant, and this is what the following context will maintain.

Jesus represents obedience to God; he stands in relationship to God in the way that the people of God are meant to. He personifies a community, Israel, and vindicates them as such by vicariously going through a death and resurrection experience on their behalf. Salvation history describes this as the act by which the commencement of the kingdom of God on earth first occurs. The vindicated Israel is now in obedience to God. Paul takes this message to the gentiles, and by their faith in the servant, the promise is now shared with them as brothers in faith, and the united house of Israel becomes the idealized community that will have dominion and come to represent the physical presence of Jesus in the future.

The Son of Man in Daniel

AUTHOR, AUDIENCE, DATE, PURPOSE

IN THIS SECTION, I turn again to Ginsberg to help expound the critical information necessary to develop the perceptual position I am proposing. According to Ginsberg, the traditional theological interpretation is that the Book of Daniel is comprised of two parts, of which the author is the prophet Daniel and the subject is the restoration of the Jewish people after the Babylonian exile through their submission to the Seleucid and Roman empires. The first part of the book is Daniel A, which spans chapters 1–6. This part of the book describes the trials and triumphs of Daniel and his three companions. My focus in the following section will be on the second part of the book, or Daniel B. This part of the book is a first-person account of the apocalyptic revelations of the prophet Daniel. According to Ginsberg, it was accepted not only by the rabbis of the Talmudic age but also by the early church fathers that Daniel B was written during the last years of the Babylonian exile of Israel and into the first few years of the Persian restorative age.[1] This places the writing of the book between 545 and 535 BCE, or around the same time as Deutero-Isaiah in traditional theology. However, according to Ginsberg, a historical-critical view of these writings estimates that Daniel B was written by four independent authors during the reign of Antiochus IV.[2] These authors are

---

1. Ginsberg, "Book of Daniel," 421.
2. Ginsberg, "Book of Daniel," 423.

described as apocalyptists one through four, suggesting that the writing of Daniel B would have concluded some time around 165 BCE, during the reign of the Seleucid Kingdom. The view of traditionalists adheres to the prophetic nature of the text, particularly with regard to Matthew's use of Daniel's prophecy of the abomination of desolation from Dan 11:31:

> So when you see standing in the holy place "the abomination that causes desolation," spoken of through the prophet Daniel—let the reader understand—then let those who are in Judea flee to the mountains. (Matt 24:15–16 NIV)

What the writer of Matthew attempts to do here is recontextualize the historical event of the desecration of the temple during the rule of Antiochus IV (a current event in Daniel's time) to an event in Matthew's own time, the destruction of the temple during the Roman-Jewish war in 70 CE. During the Seleucid rule, the Jewish temple was paganized by the Seleucid rulers when a statue of Zeus was placed in the temple. This is what Daniel was actually speaking of at the time of his writing; however, the writer of Matthew uses this verse from Daniel to speak of the destruction of the Jewish temple in 70 CE. In light of a more traditional reading, this method expounds the prophetic nature of the texts of Daniel, which may be said to have prophesied events which occurred during the time of Jesus.

The critical view is that the content of Daniel is concerned primarily with expressing the course of history encountered by the Jewish people not only after the exile but throughout the Maccabean period as well. What we actually encounter are instructions to the Jewish community living under Greek oppression and the rule of Antiochus IV on how to persevere. It is fitting, then, that both Deutero-Isaiah and the second part of the Book of Daniel be my subject themes in this book.

A DISCUSSION OF THE RANGE OF MEANINGS OF "SON OF MAN"

According to Wenham, there is little doubt that "the sayings in the Synoptic Gospels and Revelation which refer to the son of man coming on the clouds of heaven are echoes of the Daniel 7 vision of 'one like a son of man,'"[3] the figure who comes on the clouds of heaven and to whom is given great authority and dominion. It is to be noted that there actually is a very strong case which can be presented for likening the Gospels' teaching of the kingdom of God to the Jewish eschatological hopes for the new age and the restoration of Israel. Wenham shows how in this perspective, which supports my hypothesis, "Jesus announced the arrival of that long awaited time."[4] In this way, we can contextualize our understanding of Jesus' message to understand that he was in essence the fulfillment of the Davidic covenant, or more so, of the promise that a descendant of David would rule over the house of Israel forever. In other words, he is the Holy One who rules over the kingdom of Israel, the manifestation and supreme agent of the Abrahamic covenant, the one through whom the promise originally bequeathed to the descendants of the house of Jacob was extended to all the nations of the earth. If we accept this perspective, then we can also accept that Dan 2 and 7 are the most appropriate background for the teachings of the kingdom and the son of man as explicated by Jesus in the New Testament.

With help from Hartman and Di Lella, we see that in the Book of Ezekiel, "son of man" is an expression used some ninety-three times in addressing the prophet. It is also employed fifteen other times where it is a lyrical expression for "man" in "poetic and solemn contexts" (consider Num 23:19; Isa 51:12; 56:2; Jer 49:18, 33).[5] Hartman and Di Lella further show us that the term has been used throughout the Old Testament, often singularly, and also at times collectively when pluralized to describe "men," or

3. Wenham, "Kingdom of God," 133.
4. Wenham, "Kingdom of God," 133.
5. Hartman and Di Lella, *Book of Daniel*, 85

"human beings," as in Dan 2:38 ("wherever the children of men dwell") and 5:21 ("then he was driven from the sons of men"). Essentially, it should be noted that the term is used throughout the Old Testament; however, two things in contemporary scholarship are very clear. First, as I mentioned earlier, the references to the son of man and the kingdom of God by Jesus in the New Testament are most likely references to the Danielic explications of the same term. Furthermore, the term "son of man" in Daniel is in some ways different than when the term is used in other parts of the Old Testament. Hartman and Di Lella explain that the term can best be translated as "one in human likeness" or "one like a human being."[6] They further show us that when Jesus makes reference to the son of man, most New Testament translations of the original Aramaic expression prefer the phrase "one like the Son of Man," as if the "expression were a proper designation or title of a specific historical or mythological or supernatural person of the male sex."[7] When Jesus refers to the son of man, we can assume that he is referring to the Danielic expression of the concept, but this term in this context can also refer to a specific figure in history. Hartman and Di Lella also explain how just as in Daniel the four horrifying beasts are not real beasts but are symbolic representations of the pagan kingdoms of the Babylonians, Medes, Persians, and Greeks, so too the "'one in human likeness' is not primarily an individual, celestial or terrestrial, but rather is best understood as being a symbol of the 'holy ones of the most high,'" a title that was given to the faithful Jews who withstood the persecution of Antiochus IV Epiphanes.[8]

It is asserted by James D. G. Dunn, that the Danielic figure of the son of man is the chief source for the whole son of man motif throughout the gospels.[9] While the term does appear in other parts of the Old Testament, Dunn argues that in the Jesus tradition, the other son of man texts are explained as extensions of the Danielic

6. Hartman and Di Lella, *Book of Daniel*, 87.

7. Hartman and Di Lella, *Book of Daniel*, 87.

8. Hartman and Di Lella, *Book of Daniel*, 87.

9. Dunn, "Danielic Son of Man," 542.

motif. This, coupled with Hartman and Di Lella's assertions that the figure points to the faithful Jews, will form a sort of basis for my following arguments.

DANIEL 7 AND THE SON OF MAN

Israel as the Son of Man

Concerning Daniel's description of the son of man, I estimate that this figure points to the nation of Israel personified as a righteous being, just as Israel appears as the suffering servant in Isaiah. As the son of man comes with the clouds of heaven, so Israel is shown to be the righteous one of God in contrast to those arising from the waters of chaos, or kingdoms of the earth which are against Israel (Dan 7:2–3). Like the suffering servant, the son of man figure was traditionally interpreted by Christians as Jesus in his first and second coming, both in his death and resurrection and in the imminent parousia. As this was the eminent interpretation of the early church, to this day in traditional Christian theological interpretations the person and character of Jesus are read back into the Old Testament text of Daniel. Both views are valid scholarly and exegetical approaches to interpreting Dan 7:13–14, but in the historical context of the prophetic literature itself, I estimate that the son of man figure was meant to portray the restored nation of Israel in the exilic and postexilic periods.

It is this perspective that I will hold to in this book. I will, however, show that the traditional view of the son of man as pointing to the person and purpose of Jesus, can be deepened in light of my proposed alternative reading. I estimate that the Jewish prophet Daniel was demonstrating the perfect and obedient relationship that humanity could have with God. I find that Daniel shows that "the holy people of the Most High" (Dan 7:27), who shall be given an everlasting kingdom, represent the righteous, or elect, of Israel—those who have witnessed submission to the four world empires described, either physically or spiritually, and have come unto an age of restoration in which the son of man suffered and died and was brought to life once again. The death and resurrection experience of the son of man is, in many ways, the same experience of the suffering servant of Israel, and therefore, the differences in the way the two Jewish prophecies were fulfilled by the person of Jesus are few. Because of this, I will limit this section on Daniel, as the latter section, which demonstrates how these scriptures were fulfilled in a New Testament context, will further explicate the ideas I am attempting to demonstrate.

I will begin with a brief analysis of Daniel to form a better understanding of what the message of the prophet was in his own historical context, and how Israel understood this message at the time. The next section will look at how this message reached a more abstract level in the Gospel of Matthew.

Redditt's work helps us understand how the apocalyptic worldview of Daniel arose out of the dystopia created by the Jewish exile in Babylon. The exiled Jewish community fell into a state of despair in being removed from their homeland. It seemed that the covenant promise had been broken. Some Jews in exile resorted to apocalyptic rhetoric in an attempt to deal with their current situation and envision their fate. Redditt explains how in no way was it possible for the Jews in Babylon to change the society into which they had been absorbed, and consequently, a group of depoliticized scribes began writing what is now known as exilic prophetic scripture. In this way, it is plausible that Dan 1–6 arose "among Judeans in the diaspora" and Dan 7–12 by "repatriates back in Jerusalem" who were worried about their nation's future.[10] Redditt explains how in this way, the Danielic community in question is made up of the people "most likely to cultivate and preserve narratives about Judean wise men succeeding in the court of a foreign king," and, since the setting of the book is Babylon, we "may plausibly suppose that the group lived there."[11] Redditt shows us it is clear that the Danielic community "harbored hopes of succeeding amongst the Seleucids," and the writers composed the book with the intent of

---

10. Redditt, "Book of Daniel," 321–39.

11. Redditt, "Book of Daniel," 325.

giving hope to the Jewish people living under foreign rule.[12] In this way, Daniel carries the journey of the Jews into exile and Babylon, through to the restoration of the Jewish state under the freedoms granted by Cyrus—and more importantly, by God (known as the Ancient of Days)—and into the period of Seleucid rule.

Steinmann's work helps us understand how the apocalypse contained within Dan 7 outlines the fate of the son of man through a vision revealed to the prophet. Rather than presenting a cataclysmic eschatology, here Daniel offers a vision of the future of the son of man and his relation to the regimes of the Babylonians, the Medes and Persians, the Greeks, and lastly, to the Romans. The historical context of Daniel is centered on the Babylonian dynasty. Steinmann shows us it should be noted that there is a lack of extrabiblical evidence for many of the events outlined in Daniel. However, this "lack of extrabiblical evidence . . . does not mean that (the) events and persons are fictional."[13] With help from Lucas, we can see that the historical context of Daniel is as follows: In 626 BCE, Nabopolassar declared himself king of the Babylonians and was eventually joined by the Medes in attacking Assyria. Eventually, Assyria was weakened and Judah's struggle for independence ensued. By the time of the reign of the Babylonian king Nebuchadnezzar, Assyria as well as Judah had fallen to the Babylonian forces. Lucas shows us that the initial deportation of Daniel and his people "seems to relate to the initial subjugation of Judah by Nebuchadnezzar."[14] The final surge of Judah's independence at the time was led by Jehoiachin, who also eventually surrendered to the Babylonian forces, at which point he and his family, as well as many "leading citizens and a great deal of booty were taken to Babylon."[15] Zedekiah was replaced as the ruler of Judah and by 589, Babylonian armies had seized the city. The consummation of this siege occurred in 587 BCE with the destruction of the palace and the temple. Judah no longer existed as an independent state,

12. Redditt, "Book of Daniel," 197.

13. Steinmann, *Daniel*, 11.

14. Lucas, *Daniel*, 37.

15. Lucas, *Daniel*, 38.

and the region was annexed as a part of the Babylonian Empire. Lucas shows us that all the while, tension between the Medes and the Babylonians escalated until the Persian ruler Cyrus conquered Babylon while uniting with the Medes. In 538 BCE, Cyrus "issued a decree ordering the restoration of the Jewish community and cult in Judea,"[16] as noted in Ezra 1:1–4:

> Now in the first year of Cyrus king of Persia, in order to fulfill the word of the LORD by the mouth of Jeremiah, the LORD stirred up the spirit of Cyrus king of Persia, so that he sent a proclamation throughout his kingdom, and also put it in writing, saying: "This is what Cyrus king of Persia says: 'The LORD, the God of heaven, has given me all the kingdoms of the earth, and He has appointed me to rebuild for Him a house in Jerusalem, which is in Judah. (KJV)

This event is also mentioned in Dan 6:28 ("So this Daniel prospered in the reign of Darius and in the reign of Cyrus the Persian") and also in Dan 10:1 ("In the third year of Cyrus king of Persia a thing was revealed unto Daniel whose name was called Belteshazzar" [KJV]).

Hartman and Di Lella explain how because the author describes the reigns of these world empires over the Jews, it is likely that the author of chapter 7 wrote "sometime after Epiphanes had angered the Jews by his commercial exploitation of the high priesthood of the Jerusalem Temple . . . and probably after his plundering of the Temple in 169 B.C.E."[17] Hartman and Di Lella tell us that since the prophet "does not make even an obscure allusion to the king's desecration of the Temple and the beginning of his bloody persecution of the Jews in 167 BCE (1 Macc 1:20–23), he surely did not write chapter 7 after these events."[18] With these historical events in mind, we can shape our authorship hypothesis according to these incidents. In this way, the dating of the writing of chapter 7 can safely be placed between 169 and 167 BCE.

16. Lucas, *Daniel*, 39.

17. Hartman and Di Lella, *Book of Daniel*, 214.

18. Hartman and Di Lella, *Book of Daniel*, 214.

THE TRADITIONAL THEOLOGICAL
INTERPRETATION OF DANIEL 7

By analyzing form and structure and engaging in literary criticism of a text, we can further understand the tradition within which it has arisen. Lucas shows that insofar as Dan 7 is concerned, the chapter has "the form of a symbolic vision account encapsulated in a dream report."[19] The chapter itself consists of an introduction, a report of the dream vision, the interpretation, and a conclusion. In chapter 7, if we focus on verses 13–14, the throne verse, or the climax of the scene with the four beasts, the figure of the son of man—the one like a human riding on the clouds—appears to be a supernatural being or entity. It is this figure that I argue represents the faithful of Israel after their vindication. I will now briefly demonstrate some interpretations of the son of man figure in current scholarship.

According to some scholars, the Hebrew words *adam* and *enosh* can be used to refer to all of humanity, and consequently, any human could be the "son of man." According to Yarbro-Collins, "'Son of Humanity' is a possible translation, but does not yield very good sense in English."[20] According to Lucas, the one "'like a Son of Man' means a 'human figure' seen in a vision, where the figure may or may not represent something other than a human being."[21] It is also important in an eschatological sense to note the parallels between Dan 7:9–27 and Rev 4–5. The closest parallel comes when we compare Dan 7:3 ("And four beasts came up from the sea, diverse from one another") to Rev 4:8:

> And the four beasts had each of them six wings about him; and they were full of eyes within: and they rest not day and night, saying, Holy, holy, holy, Lord God Almighty, which was, and is, and is to come. (KJV)

19. Lucas, *Daniel*, 184.
20. Yarbro-Collins, "Jesus as 'Son of Man,'" 392.
21. Lucas, *Daniel*, 184.

Steinman further notes that Daniel also "has parallels to Revelations 19–20, including the final judgment at the end of the world upon Christ's return, which still lies in the future."[22]

Steinman further shows that in the traditional theological interpretation, the four beasts in Daniel depict the "four world empires that precede the birth of Christ, which takes place during the reign of the fourth empire, Rome."[23] According to Backus, the first beast represents the kingdoms of Assyria and Babylon—he is "given a human heart and placed on his feet because of his knowledge of God."[24] The second beast is the kingdom of the Medes and the Persians, the third beast is the kingdom of Alexander, and the fourth beast is the Roman Empire, "which is immediately to precede the last judgment."[25] However, according to Steinman, with the "one like a human being," the later eschatological implications come from the connection to Rev 4–5, "a vision of the enthronement of the lamb after his victory on the cross."[26] This is an archetype that exists throughout the most careful christological and traditional readings of the text. According to Steinman, it is clear that Christians today read the text knowing that the four empires depicted in Daniel have already passed away and that Christ has already "established the eternal kingdom of God by his incarnation, life, ministry, suffering, death and resurrection."[27]

We have seen how Daniel explicitly describes the historical events which took place in Canaan and Mesopotamia around the time of the Jewish exile to Babylon. We have also come to know that the traditional Christian theological reading of the text prophetically expounds the enthronement and victory of Jesus after his death and resurrection. Still, it is possible that the christological interpretations of these scriptures may suggest something different than what these verses meant to the Jews originally being spoken

22. Steinman, *Daniel*, 329.

23. Steinman, *Daniel*, 329.

24. Backus, "Beast," 62.

25. Backus, "Beast," 62.

26. Steinman, *Daniel*, 329.

27. Steinman, *Daniel*, 330.

to in the historical context of Daniel. After the death and resurrection of Jesus, the prophetic literature not only of the exilic period but of all pre-Christian Judaism came to take on a very different meaning and role. Texts were now read christologically, with the resurrection as the culmination of all Old Testament prophecies. It is evident that reading Daniel in this way provides us with some insight into the nature of the text as a means to an end, while the far-reaching implications of this book still remain today in regard to its eschatological and archetypal dimensions.

AN ALTERNATIVE INTERPRETATION OF DANIEL 7

In our interpretations of the son of man figure in Daniel, we can explore various methodologies to understand who this figure is and how he relates to different contextual viewpoints. It has been shown that in the traditional Christian interpretation, the son of man figure is understood as the person of Jesus; it is taken as symbolism of his imminent second coming. However, according to Hartman and Di Lella, in the historical context of the Jewish exile in Babylon, the son of man figure was a "representative of the 'holy ones of the Most High,'"[28] particularly as seen in Colpe's first stage of interpretation.[29] Hartman and Di Lella show that according to Colpe, the son of man refers to the angelic host whose "role in the end time will extend also to earthly empires."[30] In the second stage of interpretation, however, these "holy ones of the Most High" become "the faithful Jews who were persecuted by Antiochus IV," and the "one in human likeness" is "to be taken as a symbol of the Israel of the faith which will replace the pagan empires."[31] In both stages of interpretation, however, the "one in human likeness" is

---

28. Hartman and Di Lella, *Book of Daniel*, 89.

29. Carsten Colpe, "ho huios tou anthropou," in Friedrich, *Theological Dictionary*, 415–19.

30. Hartman and Di Lella, *Book of Daniel*, 89.

31. Hartman and Di Lella, *Book of Daniel*, 89.

a "collective person with a saving eschatological function."[32] This interpretation sits favorably in my proposed reading of the text, as it demonstrates how the "Israel of the faith" will reenter a state of obedience to God. Zevit favors the opinion that the "one in human likeness" is the angel Gabriel, who represents the "holy ones of the Most High," or the Jewish people in the kingdom of the future.[33] Again, Zevit's argument is in harmony with my reading of the text, as it allows us to understand "son of man" as a collective term for a righteous community in obedience to God. This community has an eschatological function that is both realized and futurist, and I will explore this idea in a later section.

According to Collins, this figure in Dan 7 symbolizes "primarily the angelic host and its leader (Michael) but also the faithful Jews in so far as they are associated with the heavenly host in the eschatological era."[34] This interpretation "cannot be established conclusively from the usage of the term 'holy ones' in Jewish writings but emerges from the parallelism between the various sections of the Book of Daniel itself."[35] Here again we see that Collin's reading is in harmony with mine, as he also shows that the son of man is a collective group with a saving eschatological function. Traditionally, "son of man" in this way can be seen to be a term that was synonymous with the righteous of Israel. Later, we will see how this community came to include the faithful of the gentile world who also entered into an obedient relationship with God by their faith in the death and resurrection experience of the servant and son of man personified in Jesus. The view of Collins that the "son of man" and the "holy ones" are primarily angelic beings in Daniel corresponds with the "expectation of a heavenly savior, accompanied by his host elsewhere in intertestamental and NT works."[36] These viewpoints are part and parcel of my view that the son of man represents the righteous of Israel in an idealized, eschatological

32. Hartman and Di Lella, *Book of Daniel*, 89.
33. Zevit, "Structure and Individual Elements," 396.
34. Collins, "Son of Man," 66.
35. Collins, "Son of Man," 66.
36. Collins, "Son of Man," 66.

sense—in that they symbolize the community of the faithful who will act as a light to the nations and collectively embody the person of Jesus in the second coming, just as he personified Israel in their vindication.

In Dan 7:13–14, the prophet describes the restoration of Israel to "dominion, glory and a kingdom" (7:14) because of the ancient one's intercession in destroying the fourth beast:

> I kept looking in the night visions, and behold, with the clouds of heaven one like a son of man was coming, and He came up to the Ancient of Days and was presented before Him. And to Him was given dominion, honor, and a kingdom, so that all the peoples, nations, and populations of all languages might serve Him. His dominion is an everlasting dominion which will not pass away; and His kingdom is one which will not be destroyed. (Dan 7:13–14)

It is clear that the prophet is writing about the restoration of Israel due to the intercession of God, or the "Ancient of Days," and it is possible to see how this text was used by Christians to describe the intercession of their savior, Jesus Christ. I argue that the restoration of the righteous of Israel as a holy nation is the primary meaning of this text and will examine this idea in the next section. The role of Jesus as the son of man and suffering servant in his death, resurrection, and cosmic return in judgment will be reviewed in the next section as well, considering most fundamentally that through a synthesis of interpretation, Jesus represents Israel both as the suffering servant and as the son of man personified in his character.

Messianism Realized in the Gospel of Matthew

The Sacrifice of Jesus

THE IMAGES OF THE SON OF MAN AND THE SUFFERING SERVANT INTERPRETED IN THE LIFE OF JESUS

The Passion of Matthew and a Jewish Messiah

IN THIS SECTION, I will work through an interpretation of how the evangelist Matthew shows that Jesus represented the personification of the ideal faith congregation in direct obedience to God. Since the prophets of the Old Testament shaped their view of a righteous and faithful community with reference to their own nation, Israel, there are times when I analyze Jesus' death and resurrection as the vindicating acts by which Israel reentered into an obedient relationship with God. However, a modern universal perspective proposes that Jesus' saving eschatological function was not limited to only the people of Israel; rather, his death and resurrection were the liberating acts for the entire (worldwide) community of believers who entered into the "new" covenant relationship. In this perspective, the new community—made up of all those who, by the death of the servant, have become the elect of God—will comprise the kingdom of Heaven on earth when it is brought to full fruition. At this time, the community of the elect will assume the role pioneered by Jesus and represent his physical presence, entering into a glorified state of obedience to God. I estimate that we see this perspective in Matthew's Gospel.

Matthew shows that these elect of the Lord, or righteous of Israel, are given this place firstly because of the initial promise of God to Abraham and to Israel (through the original covenant), and secondly because of the restoration of the covenant through the true and singular personification of servant Israel, Jesus. Moving outside of Matthew's Gospel, we see this principle extended because of the discipleship of the apostles and Paul, who took this message to the world and to those of the new house of Israel, who became brothers in faith through the newly restored covenant. This idea in essence represents Conzellman's view of salvation history, which I will discuss in a later chapter. Here, I explore the Gospel of Matthew and the person of Jesus as a personification of true Israel and as the realization of the prophetic traditions behind the suffering servant of Isaiah and Daniel's son of man. I will explore the authorship and background of the Gospel of Matthew in the next chapter, where I will discuss in detail how our interpretations of the intended audience of this Gospel can affect our understanding of Matthew's context and purpose.

The passion narrative of Matthew and his account of the final moments of Jesus' life bear many similarities to the other New Testament Gospel accounts. However, there are some differences in Matthew's account which add to our understanding of the event. It is evident that all of the passion narratives follow the same basic structure. They all begin with Jesus' preparation for his own death, in which he shares with his disciples all that will happen in the coming days: "You know that after two days is the Passover, and the Son of Man will be delivered up to be crucified" (Matt 26:2). After narrating Jesus' prophecy of his betrayal by Judas Iscariot and his impending death, Matthew's Gospel then goes on to depict Jesus' trial and ultimately, his death: "Now as they were eating, He said, 'Assuredly I say to you, one of you will betray me.'" (26:21) In the traditional Christian interpretation, the prophet Jesus emphasizes to his disciples, as Matthew does to his audience, the importance of his death in its function of atoning sacrifice and what it means to the world. To touch on this briefly for a moment, according to traditional Christian theology, without the sacrificial death of Jesus on the cross, humanity would never have been redeemed from the effects of the sins of Adam. In that case, all humanity would continue to be born into sin with no hope of redemption or reunion and a true relationship with God, the Father. In this passage, there is also the thematic element of Jesus' rejection by those of his generation and their sacrifice of his innocent blood without regard for truth. This, too, was something that was a necessary feature of Matthew's explanation of the significance of Jesus' death.

I suggest that we should also consider the typically Matthean perspective of Jesus' role as the personification of Israel as the Jewish Messiah, and of his death and resurrection as the redeeming act by which Israel would be restored: "But you, Bethlehem, in the land of Judah, are not the least among the rulers of Judah; for out of you shall come a ruler who will shepherd my people Israel" (Matt 2:6). Also, we hear Jesus' proclamation after his arrest: "Nevertheless, I say to you, hereafter you will see the Son of Man sitting at the right hand of the Power, and coming on the clouds of heaven" (Matt 26:64). Herein Matthew shows us Jesus' awareness of the prophetic tradition. Jesus understands the son of man as Israel, acts as the personification of the house of Jacob, and undergoes the nation's death and resurrection so that they may experience their consequent redemption: "How then could the scriptures be fulfilled, that it must happen thus?" (Matt 26:54). In this way, the death and resurrection of Israel as a *community* is actualized by Jesus the *individual* in order to lead Israel to the point of fulfillment in their divinely appointed role as a "light to the nations" (Isa 42:6; 49:6), as had been foretold in Isaiah and Daniel and other Old Testament prophets.

The theme of a redemption of Israel is declared throughout the Old Testament—for example, the initial restoration of Israel after the captivity in Babylon is mentioned in Jer 29:14:

> "I will be found by you," declares the LORD, "and will bring you back from captivity. I will gather you from

all the nations and places where I have banished you,"
declares the LORD, "and will bring you back to the place
from which I carried you into exile." (NIV)

In order to further explicate my view, we may also see that in the
Old Testament, Isa 11:11 speaks about a restoration of Israel which
will happen a second time—the first time was after the Babylonian
captivity, and we may understand the second time in light of my
proposed reading:

> In that day the Lord will reach out his hand a second time
> to reclaim the remnant that is left of his people from As-
> syria, from Lower Egypt, from Upper Egypt, from Cush,
> from Elam, from Babylonia, from Hamath and from the
> islands of the Mediterranean. (Isa 11:11 NIV)

While this second restoration can also be understood as the
postexilic restoration if the first restoration is understood as the
liberation from bondage in Egypt, it could also very well point to a
future figurative restoration in light of the redemptive works of the
Messiah (Rom 15:12). With regard to Isaiah's description of what
I believe to be the restorative act by which Israel would reenter
into their covenant relationship with God, we gain insight from
selected readings of Isa 53. In this chapter of Isaiah, the transgressions of the wicked are atoned for by the righteous of the house of
Israel, personified by the Messiah, Jesus:

> Therefore I will give him a portion among the great,
> and he will divide the spoils with the strong,
> because he poured out his life unto death,
> and was numbered with the transgressors.
> For he bore the sin of many,
> and made intercession for the transgressors.
> (Isa 53:12 NIV)

As I mentioned in the previous chapter on Isaiah, I believe that
here we see a portrait of the restoration of the righteous of Israel to
a glorified and full membership with all of God's people in a relationship of obedience to him, and I suggest it is Israel being spoken
of in a personified way. I have also mentioned earlier (chapter 3)

how Daniel explores a similar idea of a restoration of God's people to a relationship of obedience.

It is likely that Matthew's audience is Jewish Christian (see chapter 5) and the evangelist writes in continuity with the prophetic traditions of Jewish scripture to proclaim Jesus as the Messiah of the Jews. In this way, it would be necessary for the nation of Israel to be brought into their divinely appointed role as "light to the nations" through their fulfilled union with God as the rightful heirs to the covenant promise and blessing, as the collective son of man. This is an interesting perspective—to not only consider Jesus as the Messiah of the Jewish people but to further consider the future exaltation of the restored Israelite nation as the manifestation of the second coming of the son of man.

I will explain what I mean. First, since during Jesus' lifetime Jesus represented Israel and so *was* Israel, therefore, through Jesus' death and resurrection, the relationship between Israel and God was restored. Second, the reference to the son of man coming with great power and glory refers to Matthew's vision of a future time when the righteous of Israel as the faithful community (portrayed as the "son of man") will come unto the world in their glorified state as a light to the nations. A more universal reading would cause us to interpret this promise as being extended to all of the house of Israel, or those who make up the community of all believers in Christ. In this way, the body of believers now embodies the person of Jesus, just as Jesus personified the faithful of Israel in their vindication.[1] In essence, the second coming and the enthronement of the son of man may be understood as the coming of an idealized community, present in an age where they may act as a beacon of hope to all the nations of the world. We may interpret this in the following way: Jesus, as an individual, fulfills the revelations of the Jewish prophets and begins the process of God's people reentering into an obedient relationship with him. The second part of this process is that the community of God's people, Israel, follows in the footsteps of Jesus and fills the role that Jesus first pioneered.

1. I am indebted to Dr. Adrian Leske and Dr. Steven Muir for their guidance in understanding this perspective and insight.

Considering Jesus' role as a pioneer and forerunner of the relationship of God's people to him and the representation, or personification, of what Israel was to be and later became through him, we may look into the Epistle to the Hebrews in the New Testament. This book describes Jesus role as the "forerunner" of a relationship of obedience to God on behalf of God's people:

> We have this hope as an anchor for the soul, firm and secure. It enters the inner sanctuary behind the curtain, where our forerunner,[2] Jesus, has entered on our behalf. He has become a high priest forever, in the order of Melchizedek. (Heb 6:19–20 NIV)

Part and parcel of my view is the idea described in the Epistle to the Hebrews of Jesus as not only the pioneer of our salvation but also as the finisher of the process by which the restoration was completed:

> Fixing our eyes on Jesus, the pioneer and perfecter[3] of faith. For the joy set before him he endured the cross, scorning its shame, and sat down at the right hand of the throne of God. (Heb 12:2 NIV)

In this way, we can recognize that the author of the Epistle to the Hebrews is voicing an idea that resonates with my view of Matthew's intent, which I will now further describe.

THE PASSION NARRATIVE

Matthew's passion narrative begins with the section Matt 26:2–56, wherein the initial preparations are laid out and the foundations of the Christian theology regarding the death of Jesus are put in place: "The Son of Man indeed goes just as it is written of him" (Matt 26:24). This is highlighted by the anointing of Jesus for death

---

2. The Greek term here is *prodromos*, which is a term for the high priest, who enters into the holy of holies once a year to offer a sacrifice on behalf of Israel. Literally, however, *prodromos* means "the one who runs/goes before (others)," and for this reason is important to consider here.

3. Greek: *archegon* (leader, founder) and *teleiooten* (finisher, completer).

in 26:6–13. During this section, at the Lord's Last Supper, Jesus not only shares with the disciples the intention and purpose of this final Passover meal but describes its meaning in relation to the new covenant with God which is realized through the sharing of his blood and body and which is sanctified in his death.

This section of the narrative then goes on to the most theologically important discourse in Christian doctrine. In Matt 26:26–30, Jesus explains the concept of atonement for sacrifice in relationship to the new covenant and the meaning of his death: "For this is My blood of the new covenant, which is shed for many for the remission of sins" (26:28). The idea of the new covenant traces back to the prophets again—this time to Jeremiah, who speaks of the new relationship that Israel will have with God in the near future:

> Behold, the days are coming, says the Lord, when I will make a new covenant with the house of Israel and with the house of Judah— not according to the covenant that I made with their fathers in the day that I took them by the hand to lead them out of the land of Egypt, My covenant which they broke, though I was a husband to them, says the Lord. But this is the covenant that I will make with the house of Israel after those days, says the Lord: I will put My law in their minds, and write it on their hearts; and I will be their God, and they shall be My people. No more shall every man teach his neighbor, and every man his brother, saying, 'Know the Lord,' for they all shall know Me, from the least of them to the greatest of them, says the Lord. For I will forgive their iniquity, and their sin I will remember no more. (Jer 31:29–31)

It is evident here that eschatological implications exist in Jesus' declaration that his blood is shed for the sins of all and furthermore, that he will not partake in the pleasures of life, as symbolized by wine, until the kingdom of the Father has been established on earth: "I will not drink of this fruit of the vine from now on until that day that I drink it new with you in my Father's kingdom" (26:29). In speaking this phrase and by the establishment of the promise of God to grant his righteous heirs entry into the kingdom, which has commenced in the present but will be completed in the future, Jesus establishes his new covenant among the disciples, a covenant that will be spread to the rest of the world through the will of the Father.

Matthew's passion account predicts Jesus' ultimate triumph in his resurrection, that the gospel will be spread to the whole world, and the great gathering and feast they will share on that joyous day in heaven (26:29). Jesus then follows by stating that the son of man will soon come with the clouds in heaven: "Nevertheless, I say to you, hereafter you will see the Son of Man sitting at the right hand of the Power, and coming on the clouds of heaven" (26:64). While the passage denotes a coming from heaven to earth, or a direction downward by the son of man, I estimate that we may consider whether Jesus is speaking of something more abstract. It is clear to me that here Jesus understands his role as the personification of the people of God in an obedient relationship with him, or, in a more continuous way, as a personification of the nation of Israel. Just as it was written in the prophets, the descendants of the house of Jacob will have to undergo a death and resurrection experience in order to be made righteous again before God, and this was symbolically completed in Israel's exile to Babylon and consequent restoration, but in a more direct way, was undertaken by the personification and idealization of their community, Jesus. Now, when the prophet, Jesus, identifies himself as the son of man, a term that was synonymous with the nation of Israel in prophetic literature, Jesus makes an eschatological prophecy that soon God's people will symbolically be seated at the right hand of God and will carry the power of the heavens within them. They will stand in relationship to the Father and to the Son in the way that the Son once stood before the Father. Once the righteous of Israel come to have faith in the vicarious suffering of Jesus the Messiah, their vindication is thenceforth complete.

Matthew suggests that the idealized community in an eschatological sense of the righteous of Israel is made up of all of those who have placed their faith in the vindication of Israel through the servant Jesus. Once this community—the faithful of the world, the sons and adopted sons of Israel—experience their enthronement in heaven, the son of man experiences his exaltation and sits at the right hand of the Father. I therefore argue that the traditional theological interpretation of these passages, which expounds a victory of the cross and the absolution of sin, is not the only interpretation of the fulfillment of the prophecies in the Old Testament. When we consider these revelations in their historical context, we can come to a clearer understanding of the person and mission of Jesus—that his role was to redeem Israel and to transfer the covenant promise to the righteous among them, those who placed their faith in the redeeming act of their Messiah.

Matthew's Vision of Hope
The Eternal Messianic Kingdom

AFTER THE DEATH OF JESUS:
THE SECOND COMING

IN THE LAST CHAPTER, I showed how the presentation of Christ's passion in the Gospel of Matthew describes the restorative act by which Jesus, standing in direct obedience to God and exemplifying the ideal covenant relationship of his people, goes through the death and resurrection experience which is necessary for the restoration of the righteous of Israel, as spoken of by the prophets. Jesus goes through this experience on behalf of his nation as a singular personification of the people of God as a *microcosm* in order to vindicate the house of Israel and all those who place their faith in this act of justification—or, in other words, the people of God as a *macrocosm*.

In the following section, I will describe in detail how the portrayal of the messianic kingdom in the Gospel of Matthew provides further evidence for my argument. We have seen that the Jewish prophets were given revelation into the state of an ideal community living in direct obedience to God, and that they sometimes spoke of that community as a collectively personified individual. I will now show that the writer of Matthew developed this concept by portraying Jesus as the embodiment of true Israel. The Gospel writer shows how Jesus enacted the relationship of Israel in complete obedience to God; and by going through the death and resurrection experience that was required for his nation to reenter into a restored relationship with God, Jesus commenced a definitive new phase in the history of the house of Jacob. I will demonstrate how Matthew presented Jesus as performing a saving, eschatological function that was both realized and futurist, individual and social.

The social element of this eschatology is as follows. The old covenant relationship between Israel and YHWH had as its marker the complete obedience of the Jews to the will of God. But, as a result of their defiance, this covenant had been broken. Jesus, as the fully obedient Son of God, was also a social eschatologist who brought to the Roman-occupied Israel-Palestine of the first century the changes necessary in society to restore the relationship between humanity and God.[1] This is why the new covenant for the righteous of Israel was passed to all people who placed their faith in the death and resurrection experience of the embodiment of true Israel as personified by Jesus.

It is necessary for me to speak on the authorship and writing of Matthew in order to support my argument. Matthew was written originally for a Jewish Christian audience, and this sort of audience would have been receptive to the discovery of a relationship of humanity in complete accordance to the will of God. Here, the macrocosm of humanity to God stands in parallel with the microcosm of Jesus' personal relationship with YHWH.

THE HISTORICAL CONTEXT OF THE GOSPEL OF MATTHEW

Matthean Background: Purpose and Intent

The colors of faith groups can be said to change with respect to the social climate of the time in which they exist, and it is necessary to keep this in mind when considering the Gospel of Matthew. In this section, I will draw primarily from the work of the late Rabbi

---

1. I will discuss some of these social changes in the next chapter.

Daniel Jeremy Silver in helping us understand the necessary context.[2] Rabbi Silver helps us see how the winds of the Jewish faith during the historical era of Matthew were blowing over rocky and violent terrain. He shows us that the Hasmonean dynasty which came into power after the Maccabean revolt in 164 BCE had just come to an end after the ill-advised attempt of John Hyrcanus II to gain control over the Jewish autonomous state by bringing Roman influence into Jewish society. In an attempt to overthrow his brother Aristobulus II, who had made himself both high priest and king, Hyrcanus asked for General Pompey and his army to come to his aid. The result was the overthrow of Aristobulus II and the installing of Hyrcanus as high priest and ethnarch. However, Rome would now control the once-Jewish state and was responsible for electing all subsequent figureheads. In essence, this led to the cessation of the Jewish state to Roman authority.[3]

Rabbi Silver explains how by the time of Jesus' birth around 5 BCE, the Jewish state was administered by Herod the Great. While the Jews were symbolically in control of their homeland, it was to the dismay of the Torah-observant population that the ruling ethnarch was only socially identifiable as a Jew—in reality, he was ethnically an Idumean. Silver explains that Herod the Great was a capable but ruthless ruler, and his grandiose rebuilding of the Jewish temple and the fortress at Masada was overshadowed by his inability to trust and his devastatingly cruel demeanor. The historical context of the presence of Herod may be seen early in Matthew's Gospel. Consistent with his psychological shortcomings, Herod's fear of being overthrown led him to slaughter all male children under the age of two in Bethlehem:

> Then Herod, when he saw that he was deceived by the wise men, was exceedingly angry; and he sent forth and put to death all the male children who were in Bethlehem and in all its districts, from two years old and under, according to the time which he had determined from the wise men. (Matt 2:16)

2. Silver, *History of Judaism.*

3. Silver, *History of Judaism,* 180–87.

Rabbi Silver further shows how it is evident that during the time of the writing of Matthew, Jews were being marginalized by power-seeking authorities.[4] Furthermore, any hopes they had for the return of a Davidic kingdom were hardly being brought to fruition. Matthew paints a vivid picture through the use of tense language and symbolism, allowing his audience to picture the shortcomings of the governing authorities with regard to the stability of the Jewish populace at large, as well as to the followers of Jesus. We can also see here that the historical context of the events and entities that existed around the time of Jesus can be validated through the interconnecting of Mediterranean history and the stories in the New Testament.

Along with being influenced by (as well as addressing) the current state of the Jews in the Roman Empire, Matthew is heavily influenced by the Jewish prophetic tradition. The Gospel attempts to show that Jesus is a Davidic heir while demonstrating that the messianic expectations of the Jews have been fulfilled through his work, life, and ministry. Matthew's implied use of prophetic expectations from the Old Testament, and his attempts to foster the notion that Jesus is the fulfillment of all such hopes, is a predominant theme throughout his Gospel. The demonstration of evidence in support of this notion is interwoven throughout the entire text, and this provides considerable substantiation for the fact that the Matthean audience was primarily made up of Jewish followers of Jesus. We see that the message of Jesus fulfilling messianic expectations is, in this context, being addressed to an audience who took seriously prophetic and Torah traditions. An example of Matthew's demonstration of Jesus' fulfillment of Isaian prophecies may be seen when we examine how Matthew relates the passion of Christ beginning in Matt 27 to the description of the suffering servant in Isa 53:

> Surely he has borne our griefs
> And carried our sorrows;
> Yet we esteemed Him stricken,
> Smitten by God, and afflicted.

4. Silver, *History of Judaism*, 180–87

> But He was wounded for our transgressions,
> He was bruised for our iniquities;
> The chastisement for our peace was upon Him,
> And by His stripes we are healed. (Isa 53:4–5)

All of Isa 53 portrays the nature and the course that the suffering servant of Israel will experience some day in the future. In the passion account, Matthew paints a picture of Jesus as the suffering servant. Matthew also quotes several other Old Testament prophets throughout this section of his Gospel. The most vivid use of such an image of suffering occurs when Jesus is upon the cross and calls out *"Eli, Eli, lama sabachtani,"* which is also found in Ps 22:1 and is translated as "My God, My God, why have You forsaken me?" All such references to the Old Testament provide the necessary evidence to prove Jesus' fulfillment of prophecy and his messianic authority. They also provide insight into the link between Matthew and the Old Testament, and the perspective that the Matthean audience is Jewish.

Matthew ultimately wants to demonstrate to the Jewish people that Israel is to be a light to the nations of the world, and that through the vicarious death of Jesus on their behalf, the relationship between Israel and God has been restored. Jesus as the personified suffering servant restores the house of Jacob to its place as an exalted nation, but now it is only through the acceptance of Jesus as the Jewish Messiah that this renewal can take place. As a result, the promise of this restored relationship is passed on to the righteous of Israel who have accepted Jesus as their Messiah, and also to those who have become the adopted sons of Israel—those who are not Jewish by ancestry but who have similarly accepted Jesus as their savior and God's envoy. In this way, the idea I expressed in the earlier chapter on Isaiah resonates here—that according to the exilic prophets, only a remnant of Israel would emerge from the history that was brought unto them.

MATTHEW: JEWISH OR GENTILE AUDIENCE

An Evangelical Audience

The fulfillment of Old Testament prophecy is a major theme in Matthew's Gospel: "Do not think I have come to abolish the Law or the Prophets; I have not come to abolish but to fulfill" (Matt 5:17 NIV). This remains the basis of Jesus' entire purpose and is our link to questions related to authorship and audience. It is clearly indicated again in Matt 26:54–56 that the primary audience of this Gospel are Jews with messianic expectations when Jesus says: "How then would the scriptures be fulfilled, which say it must happen in this way? . . . All this has taken place so that the scriptures of the prophets may be fulfilled" (NASB).

O'Rourke helps us see how arguments that support the intended-Jewish-audience hypothesis would note that Matthew's use of the Septuagint's Greek scriptures is most often validated by his desire to express continuity with the Old Testament, and he often shifts between using the LXX and the original Hebrew scriptures as he sees fit to present his views. Herein we see Matthew's interest in declaring to the Jewish people that Jesus is their Messiah, the one who will represent their nation as a whole and bring them into the new covenant relationship as described in Jer 31. In essence, Matthew uses Old Testament texts presupposing the following ideals: "literal fulfillment, typical sense and accommodation."[5] In other words, Matthew uses the Old Testament texts to show (1) that Jesus is the literal fulfillment of the prophets and (2) that these prophecies can be directly interpreted in their meanings to be an explanation of Jesus' role and person, and he uses the different versions of the Hebrew scriptures interchangeably to accommodate what he is trying to show his audience. In essence, the Old Testament is used as a literary source to clearly charge his audience with accepting the authority of Jesus as the Jewish Messiah—the representation of what true Israel is to be.

5. O'Rourke, "Fulfillment Texts," 401.

It is part and parcel with my proposed hypothesis that Matthew is addressed to a "local community," or Jewish audience. According to Ulrich and some other scholars, however, this "local community hypothesis has tended to obscure evidence that does not fit within the frame."[6] In other words, it occurs that "many sayings attributed to Jesus seem more relevant for the audience *of* the story than for the audience *within* the story."[7] Here, the audience *of* the story can be said to be an evangelical or missionary society of believers, as opposed to the Jewish audience of Jesus *within* the gospel. While it is most certainly evident that Matthew's Gospel is addressed to his immediate Jewish audience, it is interesting to note that there exists another side to this debate which proposes that Matthew is also addressed to the later audience of the story, the ones who would come to read his Gospel after many Jewish people had already embraced the new covenant relationship through Jesus. This audience represents an expansion of the faithful of Israel, including those brothers in faith of the gentile world, who have entered into the covenant promise in the way the prophets had described—humanity in complete obedience to the will of God. While the Jewish-audience hypothesis (the audience *in* the story) is the most widely circulated, there is another possibility—that of Matthew's ultimate audience being a later representation of all followers of Jesus, or those well aware of their mission to bring the message of the new covenant of the righteous of Israel to the nations of the world. I suggest that this is the ultimate perspective Matthew attempts to create in his readers.

Ulrich also helps us consider this by examining sections such as Matt 10:37–38: "Then He said to his disciples, 'The harvest truly is plentiful, but the laborers are few. Therefore, pray the Lord of the harvest to send out laborers into His harvest'" (NKJV). When this section is compared to other evangelical discourses from Matt 9:35–10:42, we begin to see the writer's interest in evangelism, to the extent that his ultimate audience can be seen to include gentile converts to Christianity and not only Jews whose messianic hopes

6. Ulrich, "Missional Audience," 64.

7. Ulrich, "Missional Audience," 65

have been fulfilled. While the audience within the text is a Jewish one and it is most consistently argued that Matthew was written for Jews, we may go further in our consideration. If it cannot be presupposed that Matthew's immediate audience was a gentile, Christ-following, and evangelizing audience aware of its mission to perpetuate the promise of the new covenant and of a society in obedience to the will of God, such an audience can at least be extrapolated from some of the mentioned arguments.

Ulrich also shows us how in Matt 24:14 and Matt 26:13 there occur two "predictions" from Jesus pertaining to evangelical activity. Firstly, he states that "this gospel of the kingdom will be preached in all the world [*ta oikoumene*] as a witness to all the nations [*ta ethnesin*], and then the end will come" (Matt 24:14). Note that here, the phrase "witness to the peoples" is a part of Isaiah's servant theology (Isa 55:4; 43:8–10). When mentioning the woman who has just poured fragrant oil over him, Jesus says, "Assuredly, I say to you, wherever this gospel is preached in the whole world, what this woman has done will also be told as a memorial to her" (Matt 26:13). Ulrich shows us that based on these two sayings of Jesus, we can see that the author of Matthew "expected 'this gospel (of the kingdom)' to be proclaimed to an ethnically diverse audience throughout the known world."[8] That he expects his audience to extend beyond simply the Jews of Israel is apparent here. So it may be considered to what extent the Matthean audience is Jewish and to what extent Matthew has tried to convince them that their restoration as an exalted nation will be realized through their subsequent faith in the sacrifice of Jesus; and to what extent the audience is made up of non-Jewish Christian converts who are now given the promise of the new covenant and who, in becoming the righteous of Israel, will live in complete obedience to the will of God.

Two hypotheses have been looked at thus far, one maintaining that the audience is primarily a Jewish one and the second stating that the audience is a diverse and global community. When considering the second alternative, we must reflect on the evolving

8. Ulrich, "Missional Audience," 69.

state of such literature and that Matthew, as an author of revealed Scripture, possessed the insight to foresee a later audience after the spread of Christianity throughout the rest of the Mediterranean and the world—especially considering that most scholars, including Robertson, believe Matthew to have been written some time after the letters of Paul (48–62 CE) and his mission to evangelize Israel, Turkey, Greece, and Italy, placing the dating of Matthew sometime around the 80s CE.[9]

Ultimately, if we consider that Matthew's audience is Jewish and that this is the argument which best fits within our proposed hypothesis, then Jesus, as the Jewish Messiah, suffered and died on behalf of Israel to restore them to their rightful place as the light to the nations. But the global element of this message, which relates back to the authorship hypothesis, is that this promise was passed on to the faithful of Israel—those Jews who accepted Jesus as their Messiah and, by extension (according to the *Heilsgeschichte*, or saving history of God), those gentiles who accepted Jesus as their Messiah and became the adopted sons of Israel. Matthew's Gospel best supports this argument through his emphasis on Old Testament continuity in a very historical-critical way.

It should also be noted that an analysis of authorship and audience is essential to an understanding of Matthew's presentation of the parousia, because that background allows one to understand how the prophetic material was interpreted by the New Testament writers. The fact that Matthew is addressed to a Jewish audience is important for us because it clearly shows that the Old Testament prophetic traditions were used in order to show the Jews of the time that Jesus was the Messiah they were expecting.

AUTHORSHIP AND PERSPECTIVE IN MATTHEW

Background to Matthew

As mentioned earlier, the traditional theological interpretation accepts the apostolic authorship and the canonized order of the

9. Robertson, *Gospel According to Matthew*, 25.

Synoptic Gospels. According to Derickson, however, "evangelicals' experimentation with critical methodology has resulted in questions being raised about long-held viewpoints regarding the priority of Matthew as the first Gospel to be written and about whether Matthew himself actually wrote the Gospel."[10] A difference lies between exegesis of the text in light of its initial audience and later hermeneutical interpretation in light of later audiences.

According to the traditional school of thought, rooted in acceptance of the canonical process, the Gospel of Matthew is believed to have been written by Matthew himself, an apostle of Jesus who was once known as Levi, a tax collector: "As Jesus passed on from there, He saw a man named Matthew sitting at the tax office. And he said to him, 'Follow Me.' So he arose and followed Him" (Matt 9:9). While Matthean authorship was accepted by the authoritative church fathers,[11] it has been to some extent a rejected hypothesis by some New Testament scholars. This is primarily due to the acceptance within scholarly circles of the Mark-dependent hypothesis. If one was to examine both approaches to Matthean authorship, it becomes apparent that such a paradox does not only exist within a scholastic realm, but rather, the distinctions one chooses to make in such a fundamental component of understanding Matthew result in inherently different outcomes at a very personal level to the audience of the text.

Adrian Leske helps provide further context here. If we consider the apostolic authorship claims of the church fathers, there is a considerable amount of evidence to support this argument. We must note that the account of the calling of Matthew is of utmost importance, as he is only one of the first five disciples whose calling

10. Derickson, "Matthean Priority/Authorship," 87.

11. "Of Matthew he [Papias] has stated as follows: 'Matthew composed his history in the Hebrew dialect, and every one translated it as he was able'" (Eusebius, *Ecclesiastical History*, 3.39.127). Many of the early church fathers, including Irenaeus, Tertullian, and Origen, supported the theory of apostolic authorship for the Gospel of Matthew. Papias's claim that the writer is Matthew (though the meaning of his exact quote is widely debated by many contemporary scholars today) may be one of the first and main sources of evidence that formed a basis for these early theories.

is mentioned. Leske shows that furthermore, the fact the Matthew was a tax collector is made available to us within the context of the text, and that he led "other Jewish tax collectors to hear Jesus" is also made known.[12] Within the text this occurs at Matt 9:10: "Now it happened, as Jesus sat at the table in the house, that behold, many tax collectors and sinners came and sat down with Him and His disciples." However, Leske explains that Matthew also does not "avoid references to tax collectors in a derogatory sense."[13] When mentioning a brother who has sinned against another, Jesus says, "But if he refuses to even hear the church, let him be to you like a heathen and a tax collector" (Matt 18:17). Leske explains that Matthew's derogatory references to tax collectors can be seen as a dichotomy: either Matthew is in a state of lament (or rejection of former ties) similar to that experienced by Paul after his conversion to Christianity, or the author was simply not Matthew the apostle. It is also to be noted that as a tax collector, Matthew would have had to be "fluent in Hebrew, Aramaic and Greek as well as familiar with Latin," and it is shown that the author does give evidence of such fluency.[14] Matthew is also referred to as Levi, which shows that "he was of Levitical descent," and this would explain Matthew's education and also the "constant use of the term 'chief priests' for the Zadokite priesthood in Jerusalem that virtually replaced the Levitical priesthood after the exile."[15] Leske further describes how Matthew is incredibly well versed in the Hebrew Bible and in biblical exegesis and notes that it is highly likely he received scribal training. It is likely he is addressing himself when he states: "Therefore every teacher of the law who has become a disciple in the kingdom of heaven is like the owner of a house who brings out of his storeroom new treasures as well as old" (Matt 13:52–53 NIV). Matthew essentially combines the new Christian doctrine with the old Judaic teachings.

---

12. Leske, "Matthew," 1256.

13. Leske, "Matthew," 1256.

14. Leske, "Matthew," 1256.

15. Leske, "Matthew," 1256.

Thus far, the sociohistorical context of the Gospel of Matthew has been brought to light. It is important, however, to understand the nuances of many of the discourses in Matthew—most specifically those that are eschatological in their function—and their relationship to Matt 24:29–31.

THE SON OF MAN AND THE SUFFERING SERVANT

In an earlier section, I described how the particular views of Hartman and Di Lella would serve to supplement my perspective. I would like to briefly describe those ideas with particular attention to the way they connect to the prophetic-fulfillment message regarding Jesus in Matthew's Gospel. Consider that in the Book of Daniel, the author refers to the great power and authority that would be given to a collective or corporate figure—as in Deutero-Isaiah with the suffering servant but in a more symbolic sense, with reference to "one like the Son of Man" (Dan 7:13). Daniel refers to the "sovereignty, power and greatness of all the kingdoms under heaven" being handed over to the "holy ones of the Most High" (Dan 7:27). Here, "holy ones" refers to the faithful, as in Isa 62:12 and 63:18 and in Zech 14:15.[16] These holy ones are described as the ones who are most faithful to the "holy covenant" (Isa 42:6; 55:3; 59:21). and to knowing their God, and who will be the ones responsible for bringing "many to righteousness" (Dan 12:3). According to Leske, and in accord with my interpretation, "these are clear allusions to the Servant in Isa 53:11."[17] The cornerstone of this idea is that the "dominion and glory and kingdom" (Dan 7:14) that they will possess forever (Dan 7:18, 22, 27) is essentially the kingdom of God, or "the reign of the Most High demonstrated in the lives of the faithful."[18] According to Leske, here the "Holy Ones of the Most High"—the corporate "son of man"—are the continuation of servant Israel from Isa 60:21: "Then all your people will

16. Leske, "Jesus as a Nazarene," 73.
17. Leske, "Jesus as a Nazarene," 73.
18. Leske, "Jesus as a Nazarene," 73.

be righteous and they will possess the land forever. They are the shoot that I have planted, the work of my hands, for the display of my splendor."

SOCIAL ESCHATOLOGY

The New Age as an Imminent Reality

"Repent, for the Kingdom of Heaven is at hand" (Matt 3:2). The voice of one crying in the wilderness is framed by Matthew as that of an insightful ascetic, someone all too aware of the immediate nature of judgment for one's actions. As an apocalyptic eschatologist, John the Baptist is portrayed as expecting a cataclysmic return of judgment by God:

> And even now the axe is laid to the root of the trees. Therefore every tree which does not bear good fruit is cut down and thrown into the fire. I indeed baptize you with water unto repentance, but He who is coming after me is mightier than I, whose sandals I am not worthy to carry. He will baptize you with the Holy Spirit and fire. His winnowing fan is in His hand, and He will thoroughly clean out His threshing floor, and gather His wheat into the barn; but He will burn up the chaff with unquenchable fire. (Matt 3:10-12)

John suggests a dramatic, even fantastic element to the nature of the appearance of the Messiah. In regard to the general and form-specific genre of apocalyptic literature, the metaphysical dimension is often an assumption of such works—a higher reality is thought to be coming to bear on this world. Here, Matthew prescribes the same sort of stylized portrayal of the impending day of judgment and renewal through John. In regard to this event, it is evident that in the apocalyptic worldview of God directing history, the cataclysmic occasion of the coming of the son of man, as in Matt 24:30, is portrayed as a crescendo that marks an end to this linear history The concept of the Messiah intersects with this apocalyptic worldview, but then it is important to acknowledge the complexity and range of Jewish interpretations relating to the Messiah and how this intricacy informs Matthew and his chosen literary audience. In Matthew, we encounter a plethora of ideas in regard to the parousia and what this conceptual idea actually means. I believe that Jesus' use of poetic discourse in Matt 24 employs language that is reminiscent of the thematic style used by the apocalyptic prophets in the Old Testament and Apocrypha. Along with this, I argue that Matthew's depiction of the parousia in chapter 24 is different than the interpretation that traditional theology holds to, particularly in regard to Jesus' expectations of the change that will happen in the new age, with an emphasis on his return from heaven, and what this actually means. Jesus uses figurative language to expand on the oral and form-specific tradition of the Jewish prophets, and his perception of worldly change, I argue, is different than what is traditionally taught in Christian theology.

It is possible that Jesus' message was overshadowed by vague and unreal expectations of the second coming by some in his context. For example, the traditional view says that the second coming of the son of man will be by the physical presence of Jesus the Messiah. I argue that what Matthew is trying to show here is that Jesus, as a social eschatologist, sought to usher in a restoration of the covenant between the new Israel and God. Matthew suggests that this covenant has extended to all people and not only those of the traditional house of Jacob, and that the community of believers is now to participate in a circumcision of the heart and a salvation through faith, acts which may supersede simply maintaining Torah obedience. With this, the commencement of the new relationship between the people and God took place, which was marked historically by a time in which the people of God entered into a state of complete obedience to him. This state of obedience to the will of God has continued to grow, both in the size of the community and the inclination of the new Israel for loyalty to YHWH. This means that the full fruition of the community and an imminent kingdom of God on earth is represented by a "realizing" eschatological scenario. The kingdom is realized, but it will come to its full fruition at some point in the future, when obedience to the will of God becomes a universal reality. This reality was first perpetuated by Israel, and now by the faithful of Israel, as shepherds of peace, the light to the nations. This is not to say that the second coming has already happened, but it also does not go so far as to campaign a cataclysmic parousia. Instead, Jesus ushers in the new era through his works and through his absolving death and resurrection, beginning the vindication and restoration of the new Israel. The full glory of the kingdom, then, is achieved through the new body of Jesus—the people of God—coming toward an age when obedience to his will becomes a universal reality and this body of the faithful assumes the role of the physical presence of Jesus, the Messiah, in the new age. This new body of the Messiah may then perpetuate the same teaching and healing that the personification of true Israel, Jesus, once did.

MATTHEW 24:29–31

The Parousia of the Son of Man

In this short section, I will turn extensively to Davies and Allison, who, in their detailed analysis of the Gospel of Matthew, explain the essence of Matt 24: "Having in verse 28, moved the mind's eye from earth to sky, the text now directs our gaze even higher. This imaginative raising of vision leaves distress behind and prepares for envisaging the good help that comes from heaven."[19] The writers describe how according to nature, the sun and moon can both be eclipsed at different times; however, here Jesus says that both "will be troubled at once."[20] Davies and Allison describe how this prophecy, "which shows that the matter of our Gospel is bound up with the meaning of the cosmos in its entirety,"[21] draws extensively from Isa 13:10: "For the stars of the heavens will be dark and their constellations will not give their light; the sun will be dark at its rising, and the moon will not give its light." Davies and Allison

19. Davies and Allison, *St. Matthew*, 357.
20. Davies and Allison, *St. Matthew*, 357.
21. Davies and Allison, *St. Matthew*, 357.

further go on to describe how related visions of the skies can be found throughout the Old Testament and intertestamental and early Christian literature. For example, Ezek 1:1 says, "In the thirtieth year, in the fourth month on the fifth day, while I was among the exiles by the Kebar River, the heavens were opened and I saw visions of God" (NIV). Davies and Allison then describe how we see similar views in Rev 4:1 and 19:11. It may be interpreted that "the lawless behavior of the heavenly bodies . . . is the sign that God has let them go, and their time is up: a new world is coming."[22] Verse 30 represents the crescendo of the coming of the son of man, "which takes place neither in desert nor inner room but is rather universally witnessed. . . . When the Son of Man finally appears, all will recognize what the church even now confesses: that he has all authority in heaven and earth."[23]

Davies and Allison further describe that in verse 31, there is the striking "absence of God the Father."[24] Rather, "the Son of Man acts completely on his own authority and sends out his angels to gather in from all the earth his elect."[25] Although the language "denotes a rapture to heaven, as in 1 Thess 4:17," it "derives from the Jewish hope that, in the later days, God would gather the Jews of the diaspora,"[26] as in Jer 29:14 and Isa 11:11. Most scholars, like Davies and Allison, assert that here, the faithful who are to be gathered could very well represent loyal Christians—as with interpretations of passages such as Ps 50:5 ("Gather My saints together to Me, Those who have made a covenant with Me by sacrifice")—but that it must be recognized that in light of Matthew's strong Jewish background, he may also be speaking "of faithful Jews being gathered from the diaspora."[27] In this way, we can see how Matthew is here directing us to what Dan 7:13–14 had initially suggested, that Israel would be restored as a light to the nations. I will maintain

22. Davies and Allison, *St. Matthew*, 358.
23. Davies and Allison, *St. Matthew*, 358–59.
24. Davies and Allison, *St. Matthew*, 362.
25. Davies and Allison, *St. Matthew*, 362.
26. Davies and Allison, *St. Matthew*, 364.
27. Davies and Allison, *St. Matthew*, 364.

that this promise has now also come to include those of the gentile world who have accepted Jesus as their Messiah and become the righteous, adopted sons of Israel. In this way, the faithful of Israel are prophesied to come in great power and glory and carry the power of heaven within them. As "faithful Israel" and "son of man" are synonymous terms, when Jesus declares the coming of the son of man, he may very well in fact be saying that the faithful of Israel will return to their place as an exalted nation and that just as he was honored for their sake, they too will be dignified in him and the new age will begin. However, now this exalted nation will be made up of only the remnant of faithful Israel, those who accepted Jesus as their Messiah and as the personification of what true Israel was intended to be.

The Kingdom of God in Luke

THE KINGDOM OF GOD AS A REALIZED EVENT

I ARGUE THAT A useful interpretation of the term "kingdom of God" as described in the Old and New Testaments as well as in the writings of Paul is that it is a portrait of the idealized community that would come to exist in a restored union with God. In this interpretation, Christians understand this relationship as being inaugurated by the death and resurrection of Jesus and their vicarious participation in that reality. This restored relationship, which will be fully realized in the community of a righteous new Israel, began through the vindication of the house of Jacob through the death and resurrection of Jesus and will come to full fruition at some time in the future. This future time will be marked by an abundance of spiritual righteousness and obedience to God, which will be shown in the exaltation and responsibility placed on the new Israel (the people or community of God). In my proposed interpretation of the significance of the person of Jesus—namely, that his death was the act by which the house of Israel was vindicated—we may explore the idea of the kingdom of God in a way that is conducive to our understanding of this approach.

In this new age of the word of God and an abundance of spiritual prosperity, the righteous that will place their faith in the one true God of the original patriarch Abraham, as well as in the suffering, death, and resurrection of servant Israel personified in the person of Jesus, will come to live in harmony with others in a social system which is united in its orientation toward God. It has been the task of this book to support the conviction of those scholars of New Testament eschatology who view the kingdom of God as realized and commenced through the death and resurrection of Jesus, and who estimate that the necessary elements for the idealized community of righteous Israel (which will come to full fruition in the future) were put in place at that time. It is through this interpretive lens that we may see the kingdom of God not simply as a place or event that will only be realized at a future period in history, but rather as an age of spiritual prosperity which was ushered in and begun during the ministry of Jesus.

The following analysis will look at this view by a consideration of the concept of realized eschatology as proposed by C. H. Dodd,[1] through the context of the Gospel of Luke, and specifically through the context of the Davidic promise of a universal savior and king. This will be examined further through the specific signs in the Gospel of Luke that the age of abundance was imminent in first century Israel-Palestine. This argument will be supported by looking specifically at the key components of the Gospel of Luke that proclaim the imminence of the kingdom of God. The apex of this argument will be that the miracle of the shared table and commensality experienced during the ministry of Jesus is a sign that the kingdom of God was already present in the age of the Messiah and his disciples and is not simply an event only to be expected at a later time.[2] This section will demonstrate how the works of Jesus and his disciples, including the miracle of the shared table, are signs that the kingdom of God was *declared* and also *commenced* at the same time in the first century.

C. H. DODD AND THE CONCEPT OF REALIZED ESCHATOLOGY

In what has since become a mainstay in contemporary studies of kingdom theology, Dodd perpetuated a theory that allowed

1. See Dodd, *History and the Gospel*.

2. The miracle of the shared table was the act of people from various social classes coming together to share a meal with Jesus and his disciples.

students of the New Testament to reinterpret one of the most central components of Jesus' parable teachings. In essence, what many would have called the unfulfilled promise of the imminence of the kingdom of God—unfulfilled throughout the works and ministry of Jesus, into early church history, and through to our present time—suddenly became understood as being a promise that commenced and was initiated at once in its declaration. Dodd argued that the kingdom of God was actualized in Jesus' ministry, arguing this on the basis of several passages in the New Testament. Sullivan shows us that Dodd first considered Matt 12:28 and argued that Jesus' declaration that he had cast out demons "by the spirit of God" indicates that the kingdom of God had most assuredly been realized: "But if it is by the spirit of God that I cast out demons, then the Kingdom of God has come upon you" (Matt 12:28 ESV).[3] Dodd further supplemented his view with evidence from Jesus' message to John the Baptist in Matt 11:4–5: "Go back and report to John what you hear and see: the blind receive sight, the lame walk, those who have leprosy are cleansed, the deaf hear, the dead are raised, and the good news is proclaimed to the poor" (NIV). According to Dodd, this passage makes it clear that the "old order closed with John; (and) the new begins with the ministry of Jesus."[4]

Sullivan explains that Dodd used these passages, along with *"The Markan Gospel Summary"* (Mark 1:14–15), *"The Beatitude of Hearing and Seeing"* (Matt 13:16–17), *"The Men of Nineveh and Queen of the South Condemnation"* (Matt 12:41–42), and *"The Violence Remark"* (Matt 11:12–13) to give evidence to his hypothesis.[5] Sullivan tells us that in all, Dodd used six passages most extensively to validate his perspective and that in his book *The Parables of the Kingdom*, he mentions that "these passages, the most explicit of their kind, are sufficient to show that in the earliest tradition Jesus was understood to have proclaimed that the Kingdom of God, the hope of many generations, had at last come."[6]

3. Sullivan, *Realized Eschatology*, 65.

4. Dodd, *Parables of the Kingdom*, 40.

5. Sullivan, *Realized Eschatology*, 66.

6. Sullivan, *Realized Eschatology*, 48–49.

SALVATION HISTORY IN LUKE

According to Conzelmann, if we consider the role of Luke as a historian, his intent clearly was to construct a *Heilsgeschichte*, or orderly account of how God acts in historical events to accomplish his will.[7] Because of this, we can infer that Luke may have attempted to demonstrate continuity in that the God of Israel is shown to be the same God who sent Jesus for the redemption of the world. Scholars like Conzelmann and Most help us to see that based on internal evidence from the third Gospel, we can make certain conclusions regarding the intellectual and social background of its author. That he possessed a great knowledge of the Jewish world and perhaps was a hellenized Jew is evident through his honoring of Hebraic heritage. This is also evident through his in-depth attention to the temple and his immense knowledge of the Septuagint. However, if we try to maintain the idea of Luke as the physician (Col 4:14), we should remember that it is most likely that such an occupation would only have belonged to a person of a Greco-Roman background. William Most explains to us that when considering the *Heilsgeschichte*, or salvation history, of Luke, it is the formal and somewhat antiquated style of the Gospel that seems to mirror the way the Septuagint may have sounded to Greek-speaking people.[8] In this way, Luke's familiarity with not only the style of the Septuagint but the language of the Greeks seems to show his attempt at creating something with a contextually and culturally relevant feel—a new sacred text that could withstand the changing face of the empire and all time.

THE KINGDOM OF GOD

The kingdom of God is an idea that is developed by the Israelite prophets in the later books of the Old Testament. I will explore how this concept relates to my work in this short section, drawing extensively on the work of B. T. Viviano to help the reader

7. See Conzelmann, *Theology of St. Luke*.
8. Most, "Did St. Luke Imitate," 31.

contextualize. This concept has since become a major theme of biblical theology and is found in passages such as 1 Chr 28:5: "Of all my sons, and the Lord has given me many, he has chosen my son Solomon to sit on the throne of the Kingdom of the Lord over Israel" (NIV). The kingdom of God is also mentioned in the Psalms and also throughout the book of Daniel, where almost every chapter "culminates in its proclamation."[9] The main references which are thought by Christians to allude to Jesus and the coming of the promised Messiah are found in Dan 7:13–14 in the proclamation that "with the clouds of heaven one like a son of man was coming" (Dan 7:13).

Viviano helps us understand how it is evident that the concepts of the kingdom of God and the Messiah are "strongly present in rabbinic literature."[10] But, as he describes, later the idea was developed in the context of contemporary Christianity to announce that the "coming of the Kingdom of God was the central message of the preaching of Jesus."[11] In the Gospel of Luke, the ministry of Jesus begins with the proclamation of the kingdom in chapter 4:18–19, which is also known as the Great Commission.

Viviano shows us how the proclamation of the kingdom is Jesus' primary focus in terms of teaching—it is the common theme of his parables, and when he shares the Lord's Prayer with his disciples, he instructs them to proclaim: "Your kingdom come. Your will be done, on earth as it is in heaven" (Matt 6:10; cf. Luke 11:2). By this, it is concluded that the kingdom has not yet been fully established on earth but "will come in its fullness in the near future, as a divine gift."[12] Still, we may observe that through the teaching and healing miracles of Jesus, the kingdom is at once already present—as in Luke 11:20, where Jesus proclaims that through the casting out of demons the kingdom of God has come upon his followers.

9. Viviano, "Kingdom of God," 172–75.

10. Viviano, "Kingdom of God," 173.

11. Viviano, "Kingdom of God," 173.

12. Viviano, "Kingdom of God," 173.

Further note that in Luke 17:20–21, Jesus declares that the kingdom is at once within us, in the midst of his followers:

> Now when He was asked by the Pharisees when the Kingdom of God would come, He answered them and said, "The Kingdom of God does not come with observation; nor will they say, 'See here!' or 'See there!' For indeed, the Kingdom of God is within you."

In this passage, we find that the kingdom of God can be interpreted in several ways and not solely as a futurist event that will commence at the return of Jesus. The kingdom is at once realized through those who participate in its message by partaking in the vicarious death and resurrection of the Messiah.

LUKE'S PORTRAYAL OF JESUS
AS THE FULFILLMENT OF ISRAELITE HISTORY

Godet helps us understand how Luke's audience appears to be knowledgeable concerning at least some of the Jewish scriptures, which is evident through Luke's use of scriptural symbolisms, particularly those pertaining to Jesus' role as that of servant Israel. It is proposed in the Lukan text that the old covenant of historic Israel has ended, and that through the death and resurrection of Jesus as a cataclysmic event, a new age of redemption has been introduced. One interpretation is that the writer of Luke was most certainly a gentile and explaining the story of how the gospel reached the rest of the world was his modus operandi. He shares Jesus' story and shows him as first quoting the prophet Isaiah to emphasize the fulfillment of Old Testament prophecies.

According to Godet, tradition claims that Luke was written by a travelling companion of Paul who probably lived in one of the cities that Paul visited. This is evident in that Luke, who also wrote Acts, mentions in Acts 16 that Paul had joined Luke and his companions in Derbe, a city south of Galatia. Godet further helps us interpret that this most likely means that Luke "had already become the companion of the apostle before he arrived in Rome" and may have taken part in Paul's missionary toils in Greece or Asia.[13] In his Gospel, he describes the story of Christianity reaching the rest of the world, a story that begins with John the Baptist and ends with the arrival of Paul in Rome. Luke's gospel also possesses the highest literary quality of any of the works in the New Testament. In regard to this, tradition maintains that Luke was a physician with a great command of Greek, which is a very important fact as it implies that Luke "possessed a certain amount of scientific knowledge, and belonged to the class of educated men."[14]

THE COMMISSION OF JESUS AND THE ADVENT OF THE MESSIANIC AGE

We can further understand the essence of Luke with regard to my research with help from Tannehill's commentary on this Gospel. In the traditional theological interpretation, the activities of Jesus represent the commencement of the Messianic age of redemption wherein the promise of a life of absolution has been fulfilled through the redeeming sacrifice of his death upon the cross. Jesus' mandate is particularly emphasized in Luke 4:18–19, which relates his reading from the scroll of Isaiah (Isa 61:1–2):

> The Spirit of the LORD is upon Me,
> Because He has anointed Me
> To preach the gospel to the poor;
> He has sent Me to heal the brokenhearted,
> To proclaim liberty to the captives
> And recovery of sight to the blind,
> To set at liberty those who are oppressed;
> To proclaim the acceptable year of the LORD. (Luke 4:18–19)

Luke's Gospel indicates that Jesus' ministry began before he returned to Nazareth, but that upon his return he had already become a well-known figure and was given the role in the synagogue

---

13. Godet, *Gospel of St. Luke*, 11.
14. Godet, *Gospel of St. Luke*, 11.

of reading and interpreting Scripture. Jesus, as mentioned in Luke 4:16, attended the synagogue every Sabbath; however, he was critical of the Jewish religious institutions of the time. This is most clearly seen in Luke 20:46, where Jesus describes the teachers of the law, who often have the "chief seats in the synagogues and places of honor at banquets." Luke also shows Jesus' view that the temple was no longer a perfect place through his turning over of the money changers' tables and his statement in Luke 19:46: "'It is written,' he said to them, 'My house will be a house of prayer; but you have made it a den of robbers'" (NIV). Luke also uses Jesus' reading of the passage from Isa 61:1–2 as a programmatic statement of Jesus' commission as the anointed one, or Messiah. In essence, this may be taken as Luke showing us Jesus' own understanding of his mission.

Tannehill explains how Jesus is later anointed with the Spirit of God (Luke 4:18) and begins the first part of his commission, which is to preach the good news to the poor. This represents the first phase in the creation of the new kingdom. The next part of his mission is to proclaim freedom to the prisoners, which—according to Tannehill—is not only accomplished literally by freeing people bound or afflicted by illness and demonic possession (see Luke 8:26–39) but also figuratively in the case of those who have suffered from social oppression because of being stigmatized.[15] Jesus and his disciples accomplished this by extending fellowship to the marginalized people of their society, as I will show later in a section on the commensality of Jesus' disciples in their preaching of the good news of the kingdom of God. Herein we find further evidence of the commencement of the eternal kingdom taking place. Jesus is also commissioned to bring recovery of sight to the blind, and while he literally does heal the blind—as seen in Mark 10:46 and John 9:1–8—there is the possible interpretation also that here the author of Luke is trying to describe Jesus' healing of those who are spiritually blind, as John shows us in 9:39–41. Thus, to "proclaim the year of the Lord's favor" (Luke 4:19), or Year of Jubilee, is Jesus' final commission in which he declares

---

15. Tannehill, *Luke*, 219.

the coming of the Messiah, who ushers in the final age wherein righteousness abounds and those who are unrighteous will suffer retribution. In the Old Testament, this Year of Jubilee is mentioned in Lev 25:8–10:

> Count off seven sabbath years—seven times seven years—so that the seven sabbath years amount to a period of forty-nine years. Then have the trumpet sounded everywhere on the tenth day of the seventh month; on the Day of Atonement sound the trumpet throughout your land. Consecrate the fiftieth year and proclaim liberty throughout the land to all its inhabitants. It shall be a jubilee for you; each of you is to return to your family property and to your own clan. (NIV)

In essence, the Year of Jubilee represents the Hebraic tradition in which the Jewish people were to count seven sabbatical years, or seven periods of seven years, and in the following fiftieth year to mark the Year of Jubilee. This year would be proclaimed on the tenth day of the seventh month, the Day of Atonement. Jesus' interpretation of the Year of Jubilee and Day of Atonement is clear in that he understands himself as the agent through whom the absolution of the Yom Kippur prayers can become manifest, through the new faith covenant which would be perpetuated through his sacrificial death. In this way, we can see that the culmination of Jesus' commission is his declaration in Luke 4:19 of the Year of Jubilee and the messianic age which is to be expected.

Through his commission and spiritual obligations to humanity, Jesus ushers in the messianic age in his own lifetime, and the kingdom of the faithful comes to be realized first through his ministry and later through the spreading of the gospel to the four corners of the earth. In this way, the kingdom of God as spoken of by Luke becomes a reality that is clear for the people of God. They have entered into a restored relationship with God marked by complete obedience to his will, and with this, the seeds of a fully realized kingdom of God have been put into place. As the faithful grow, teach, and heal on behalf of God, they come to personify the same ideals and, in some ways, the same relationship to God that Jesus had. Jesus, the personification of a collective community, stood in relationship to God in the most absolute way, and in the new age, the kingdom of the faithful now stands in relationship to God in a similarly ideal way as a communal personification of Jesus the messiah by healing, teaching, and offering his spiritual presence to the world through his word and gospel.

KINGDOM AS THE FULFILLMENT OF GOD'S PROMISE TO DAVID

The kingdom of God as proclaimed by Jesus represents an intertextual echo to earlier passages in the prophetic scriptures which allude to the kingdom of the house of David which would rule forever. This promise is made to David and declared in 2 Sam 7:13: "He shall build a house for my name, and I will establish the throne of his kingdom forever." The idea is further echoed in 2 Sam 7:16: "And your house and your kingdom shall be established forever before you. Your throne shall be established forever." In this case, Luke recontextualizes these promises as fulfilled by the person of Jesus. That the kingdom of God is no longer contained within the geographical or ethnic boundaries of Jerusalem and servant Israel but now extends to the entire world is an idea that is echoed throughout the entire text of Luke-Acts. The Davidic promise as proclaimed in Isa 9:7 is fulfilled by the person of Jesus:

> Of the increase of his government and peace
> There will be no end,
> Upon the throne of David and over His kingdom,
> To order it and establish it with judgment and justice
> From that time forward, even forever.

We see this view in Luke 1:32–33, which says:

> He will be great and will be called the Son of the Most
> High. The Lord God will give him the throne of his father
> David, and he will reign over Jacob's descendants forever;
> his kingdom will never end. (NIV)

THE PARABLE OF THE FIG TREE
AND THE IMMINENCE OF THE KINGDOM OF GOD

With help from Tannehill, I would like to briefly touch on a few examples that show the imminence of the kingdom of God as taught directly by Jesus through his sermons and parables.

The warnings in Luke 12:54–13:9 are directed to the crowds which have gathered to hear Jesus speak. The tone of voice Jesus uses in his sermon to the multitudes is harsh and judgmental, and this is the best way by which he may convey his message of urgency in repentance. Those listening to Jesus are called "hypocrites" and are blamed for failing to examine the time:[16] "You can discern the face of the sky and earth, but how is it you do not discern the time?" (Luke 12:56). In this context, it is evident that the imminent nature of judgment is the main figurative motif in Jesus' parables during this period of his ministry. At this point, it is clear that only repentance can save the people from destruction, as it is written: "Unless you repent you will all likewise perish" (Luke 13:3).

With assistance from Arthur Just as well as Norval Geldenhuys, we can understand much about the parable of the fig tree as described in Luke 13:6. We start by engaging with the idea that this parable draws on the themes previously presented in Luke chapters 12 and 13, which describe the imminence of universal judgment. We also see here that this passage refers to those who have fallen astray and have instead come now to be like the barren fig tree because of a lack of repentance. The narrative continuity in this section draws on the words spoken by John the Baptist declaring that the righteous should "bear fruits in keeping with repentance, . . . [for] the axe is already laid at the root of the trees; so every tree that does not bear good fruit is cut down and thrown into the fire" (Luke 3:8–9). Luke describes this parable as being spoken by Jesus in 13:6–9 in the following way:

> He also spoke this parable: "A certain man had a fig tree planted in his vineyard, and he came seeking fruit on it and found none. Then he said to the keeper of his

16. Tannehill, *Narrative Unity*, 151.

vineyard, 'Look, for three years I have come seeking fruit on this fig tree and have found none. Cut it down; why does it use up the ground?' But he answered and said to him, 'Sir, let it alone this year also, until I dig around it and fertilize it. And if it bears fruit, well, but if not, after that you can cut it down.'"

In this context, Jesus speaks to the crowds the same way John does, and he proclaims the urgency of his message and the disastrous consequences of failing to heed its warning.

Arthur Just shows us that the parable of the fig tree can be interpreted in several ways: the Augustinian interpretation of this story sees the tree as representing the human race, which the Lord—represented by Abraham—first visited during the time of the patriarchs in the first year of this tree. He again visited this tree during the era of the law and prophets as Moses and the Nevi'im. And now in this context, the gospel of Jesus has dawned upon the new generation, and while the tree is only fit to be cut down, the "merciful one intercedes with the merciful one,"[17] and to show his compassion, he offers to dig around it and apply nourishment of the word to its roots so that it may perhaps bear fruit.[18]

Geldenhuys explains that a second way to interpret the parable is that the tree represents servant Israel, to whom God has given every opportunity to bear good fruit. Servant Israel has not fulfilled its task, as is evident by the fact that so many have rejected the promised Messiah. Nevertheless, God has given them a third and final chance, and if they persist in their rejection of the Lord's message, they will inevitably be "cut down."

Through the death and resurrection of the chosen Messiah and through the subsequent ministry of the apostles and Paul as well as other evangelicals, the Jewish people were given several opportunities to repent; however, the majority of them refused and drew upon themselves the disasters of the Roman-Jewish war of 70 CE, wherein their national existence and identity was cut down.[19]

17. Wherein Christ intercedes with God the Father.

18. Just, *Ancient Christian Commentary*, 223.

19. Geldenhuys, *Commentary*, 372.

In studying this section of Luke, knowledge of the contextual references of the time is imperative. When attempting to understand the fate of Israel shortly after the death of Jesus, we can see that the parables contained in chapter 13 all correlate to what would become of the house of Jacob. The pattern that the writer of Luke develops in this section of his narrative of the life and ministry of Jesus takes the following structure:

1. Sin—the people fail to follow the commandments of the Lord.

2. A willingness to repent and come to the righteous word of the gospel.

3. Forgiveness—they are absolved and granted eternal life and salvation.

OR

1. Sin.

2. A failure to repent.

3. Subsequent punishment where they are kept from the kingdom of God.

While the history of servant Israel had tended to follow the latter pattern of judgment, in this final context, the writer of Luke attempts to convey Jesus' strong desire to change this pattern of punishment—with the nurturing of the Lord's gospel in their hearts—into one of eternal forgiveness through belief in a new law of faith. The author uses the very common symbolic element of the fig tree, which was commonly found in the orchards of fertile Palestine, to convey to the readers a message that is easily understood in their agricultural context.

The author of this narrative uses several literary techniques to convince the reader of his message. He foreshadows the imminent kingdom of God and subsequent judgment of the unrighteous. He alludes to the symbolism of the fig tree and uses the irony evident in the mercy of the compassionate one who convinces the owner of the vineyard, in whose hands the fate of the tree is placed, to allow him to give the tree the opportunity to bear fruit. Interwoven throughout all the parables of chapter 13 is the thematic motif of the judgment of the unrighteous and the wrath of God toward those who do not live in his favor. It is again evident here that through the compassion shown toward those who have transgressed in their faith, a final opportunity to absolve themselves simply through loyalty to the Messiah Jesus has come upon the people of Israel. This represents the descending of the heavenly realm unto earth, a realm which begins to establish its righteous influence during the life of Jesus.

MIRACLE AND TABLE—A SIGN OF THE IMMINENCE OF THE KINGDOM OF GOD

Crossan helps us to see that in accepting the invocation of God's kingdom not as "an apocalyptic event in the imminent future but as a mode of life in the immediate present,"[20] we can begin to comprehend the breadth and reach of the kingdom not only in a material sense but also in its ability to shape the hearts of all of those who are touched by its message. Through the act of sharing a table and meal with those who existed at the fringes of society in first-century Israel, Jesus ushered in a new age in which the old system of social and class differences was changed. Crossan argues that Jesus' table theology, which is powerfully symbolic, points "directly and deliberately at the intersection of patronage and clientage, honor and shame, the very heart of ancient Mediterranean society," and therefore is an integral part of his ministry.[21]

In his presentation of the sending out of the disciples, Luke offers his readers an important message of commensality among social groups:

> Then he called his twelve disciples together and gave them power and authority over all demons, and to cure diseases. He sent them to preach the Kingdom of God and to heal the sick. And he said to them, "Take nothing

20. Crossan, *Historical Jesus*, 304.
21. Crossan, *Historical Jesus*, 304.

for the journey, neither staffs nor bag nor bread nor money; and do not have two tunics apiece. Whatever house you enter, stay there, and from there depart. And whoever will not receive you, when you go out of that city, shake off the very dust from your feet as a testimony against them." So they departed and went through the towns, preaching the gospel and healing everywhere. (Luke 9:1–6)

Later, in Luke 10:4–9, a similar command is given to the seventy-two who have gathered to hear Jesus speak:

Carry neither money bag, knapsack, nor sandals; and greet no one along the road. But whatever house you enter, first say, "Peace to this house." And if a son of peace is there, your peace will rest on it; if not, it will return to you. And remain in the same house, eating and drinking such things as they give, for the laborer is worthy of his wages. Do not go from house to house. Whatever city you enter, and they receive you, eat such things as are set before you. And heal the sick there, and say to them, "The Kingdom of God has come near to you."

Crossan helps us understand how in these two sections of Luke we can begin to see the heart of Jesus' movement in his mission and message. Both sections deal with not just almsgiving but with a shared table and commensality. Both sections suggest a link between the kingdom of God and the actions of the disciples (healing, preaching, and extending fellowship), and these actions by the disciples mirror Jesus' own actions. The missionaries do not carry bags because they do not beg for alms, food, clothing, or anything else. Instead, "they share a miracle and a Kingdom, and they receive in return a table and a house."[22] And herein lies the "heart of the original Jesus movement: a shared egalitarianism of spiritual and material resources."[23] The "miracle" here is the kingdom experienced as a living reality in the simple yet profound acts of charity of Jesus and his disciples. This early mission of

22. Crossan, *Historical Jesus*, 341.
23. Crossan, *Historical Jesus*, 341.

Jesus and his missionaries represents the starting point of the later mission of Paul. Paul attempted to shatter the immense distance that existed between the major urban centers of his time by uniting them within a common fabric of Christian thought. Crossan shows us how Jesus, in order to end an old age of differences, sought to destroy the distance between people of various social positions through shared meals and spirituality—and it appears that social distance is often even more difficult to overcome than geographical distance.

The shared home and common meal must be understood in the context of the first-century Mediterranean world and through cultural studies in food and commensality. Crossan cites Gillian Feeley-Harnik, who explains that it is due to the "complex interrelationships of cultural categories that food is commonly one of the principal ways in which differences among social groups are marked."[24] In addition, Crossan cites Lee Edward Klosinski, who mentions that upon review of the most significant anthropological and sociological literature in regard to food and eating, it is evident that "sharing food is a transaction which involves a series of mutual obligations and which initiates an interconnected complex of mutuality and reciprocity."[25] Klosinski further asserts that "eating is a behavior which symbolizes feelings and relationships, mediates social status and power, and expresses the boundaries of group identity."[26]

Crossan shows us that for Jesus, commensality was not simply a strategy for the support of the missionaries and their mission, as this could have been done through alms or wages of some sort. It was rather "a strategy for building and rebuilding peasant community on radically different principles from those of honor and shame, patronage and clientage."[27] This strategy of commensal-

---

24. Crossan, *Historical Jesus*, 341.

25. Crossan, *Historical Jesus*, 341.

26. Crossan, *Historical Jesus*, 341.

27. Crossan, *Historical Jesus*, 344.

ity was based on an "egalitarian sharing of spiritual and material power at the most grass-roots level."[28]

CONCLUSIONS ON LUKE'S PORTRAIT OF THE REALIZED KINGDOM OF GOD

It was the purpose of this section to examine the nature of the kingdom of God as spoken of in the gospel of Luke. Attempts have been made to present the idea of the kingdom as established during the ministry of Jesus, a kingdom in which Christians continue to partake today through their obedience to the will of God. The commencement of the kingdom began through the atonement of Jesus and is in a consistent state of realization, both by the growth of his physical presence through the people of God and the church community of the faithful of Israel, and also by his spiritual presence in the word of the gospel. The very presence of the first-century Messiah is personified in his people, just as his role was to personify the community of faithful Israel. It is in acknowledging that the perpetuation of the kingdom of God through teaching, healing, and service is the duty of all who are a part of the covenant relationship that the new age begins to become a universal reality. Indeed, there are times when the world seems to be a great distance away from the achievement of a reality of adherence to the will of God on behalf of every person, but herein lies the original promise as made to Israel—that they would serve as a light to the nations and as shepherds of peace in the world.

---

28. Crossan, *Historical Jesus*, 344.

Conclusion

STANDING BEFORE GOD IN a relationship of complete obedience to his will—this in essence is what the Jewish prophets were speaking of as they held that template of an ideal society against the plight of their community, Israel, through their exile experience and into their restoration as a kingdom under God.

I began this book by looking at how Isaiah describes this scenario. He explains to his audience that because of the transgressions of the sinful amongst them, Israel is bound to undergo a death experience in which they will be exiled to Babylon and assigned a grave with the wicked. Isaiah describes the sufferings of servant Israel personified as a single person—the community of the faithful represented as a righteous servant of God:

> By oppression and judgment he was taken away.
>   Yet who of his generation protested?
> For he was cut off from the land of the living;
>   for the transgression of my people he was punished.
> He was assigned a grave with the wicked,
>   and with the rich in his death,
> though he had done no violence,
>   nor was any deceit in his mouth.
> (Isa 53:8–9 NIV)

Isaiah describes this death experience in detail, from the conquest by the Babylonians of Judah, into Israel's exile, and through to their restoration. While it is not difficult to interpret the whole of Isaiah, the question still lingers in contemporary theology as to who the prophet was speaking of in the context of chapter 53 and the figure of the suffering servant. I have attempted to show in my research that Isaiah was in essence speaking of the faithful of the Israelite community, here personified as a singular person. In a more abstract way, Isaiah was actually speaking about the relationship of complete obedience to the will of God on behalf of the righteous remnant of Israel that would come about, symbolized by the servant. The faithful of Israel then would eventually become God's way for establishing his eternal kingdom on earth:

> Therefore I will give him a portion among the great,
>   and he will divide the spoils with the strong,
> because he poured out his life unto death,
>   and was numbered with the transgressors.
> For he bore the sin of many,
>   and made intercession for the transgressors.
> (Isa 53:12 NIV)

Here, the faithful of Israel—personified as a righteous servant of God—have gone through the suffering, death, and resurrection experience of the exile to Babylon because of the transgressions of the wicked among them. When Isaiah speaks of God giving the righteous remnant of Israel a "portion among the great," he is speaking of the commencement of the true covenant relationship between the community of the faithful and YHWH. However, this community of the righteous elect of God is not realized in the course of Israel's history—in other words, the transgressions of the wicked among them continue to build up and keep Israel from fulfilling their vocation as described in the original covenant relationship: to be a light to the nations and the shepherds of peace in the world.

In my interpretation, I have attempted to show that the figure of the servant is a singular personification of a righteous community of the faithful standing before God in a relationship of complete obedience to his will. Throughout the course of this research, I have discussed how the personification of this faithful community is used as a literary tool to describe what the ideal relationship of the people to God is. However, this symbolism reaches a higher level of abstraction in its messianic implications. While I argue that the servant is not simply an individual—it is a community spoken of in a singular way—this view does not negate the traditional Christian theological interpretation of the text. This is because Jesus understands what the Jewish prophets have written; he knows that the community of the faithful is described by the Jewish prophets through the context of their own nation, Israel. In this way, Israel is described as a singular person, a person who stands in God's favor in every way, but this becomes an unachieved reality for their community. As Jesus takes on the role of servant Israel, he becomes the personification of their community and literally goes through a death and resurrection experience, just as was spoken of by Isaiah. By doing this, Jesus redeems the community of the faithful, completely renewing and realizing their relationship with God.

I then used the text of Daniel to further describe the relationship of this righteous community to God in its complete and literal fulfillment. Daniel uses the same literary technique as Isaiah, describing the kingdom of the righteous of Israel in its fully realized sense as a singular person, the son of man. I argued that this term as used in Daniel is not employed to simply describe a single redeeming figure with a saving messianic and eschatological function but rather is a term that personifies the faithful of Israel in their final position of favor in God's sight, in an everlasting kingdom:

> In my vision at night I looked, and there before me was one like a son of man, coming with the clouds of heaven. He approached the Ancient of Days and was led into his presence. He was given authority, glory and sovereign power; all nations and peoples of every language worshiped him. His dominion is an everlasting dominion that will not pass away, and his kingdom is one that will never be destroyed. (Dan 7:13–14 NIV)

I argued that here, the community of the faithful—or, from Daniel's perspective, the righteous of Israel in a restored relationship of complete obedience to the will of God—is what is being spoken of. I used the texts of Isaiah and Daniel to explain the idea of this righteous community of believers, not only because these scriptures very clearly describe the characteristics of this community, but because they also allow us to better understand the person and mission of Jesus. I showed that while the Jewish prophets were speaking in a symbolic and idealized way of their community as a singular person, Jesus' role was then to personify this community of the righteous and exemplify the relationship they were to have with God. In this way, as the fulfillment of the texts of Dan 7 and Isa 53, Jesus was not only an individual—he became the community of the faithful personified and stood in an exemplified, or fully realized, relationship of complete obedience to God.

I then explored this concept, and how through Jesus the covenant promise reached its full fruition in that Jesus became servant Israel and literally went through the death and resurrection experience that was spoken of by Isaiah and Daniel. In his death and resurrection, he vindicated the righteous of Israel and brought the promise of the original covenant to completion.

Matthew was used to describe the commencement of this covenant relationship because it was written for the first Jewish Christians. Matthew described to them that Jesus was the fulfillment of what the Jewish community's relationship to God was meant to be. I used the concept of salvation history to bring my arguments into contemporary Christianity and into a universal interpretation by describing how the faithful of Israel were then joined by the gentile followers of Jesus, who placed their faith in his death and resurrection and became the new Israel of the faith. In essence, the new covenant community became an extension of God's plan for Israel.

Since the act by which the faithful of Israel were vindicated—the literal death and resurrection of servant Israel—represented the commencement of a righteous community of believers now standing in a perfect relationship with God, I then segued into my interpretation of how this event came to represent the realized fulfillment of the promise of the kingdom of God. I used the Gospel of Luke to further support my conclusion. This was a section rich in the salvation history of righteous Israel, and I used the idea of the kingdom of God to describe how the eschatological purpose of Jesus is fulfilled in his community of believers. In Luke's Gospel, the evangelist shows that Jesus enacted the kingdom of God in his ministry and then instructed his followers to continue in that ministry. Therefore, the expectation of the return of the son of man at a future point in history is not confined to the literal presence of Jesus. Just as Jesus personified the community of the faithful and brought them to vindication, this remnant of righteous Israel now personifies Christ and his ministry. As this community grows in faith and sincerity, so does the physical presence of Jesus through his people and the presence of his spirit through the word of the gospel.

Bibliography

Backus, Irena. "The Beast: Interpretations of Daniel 7.2–9 and Apocalypse 13.1–4, 11–12 in Lutheran, Zwinglian and Calvinist Circles in the Late Sixteenth Century." *Reformation & Renaissance Review* 3 (2000) 59–77.

Beasley-Murray, George. "The Interpretation of Daniel 7." *Catholic Biblical Quarterly* 45 (1983) 44–58.

Betz, Otto. "Jesus and Isaiah 53." In *Jesus and the Suffering Servant: Isaiah 53 and Christian Origins*, edited by William H. Bellinger and William R. Farmer, 70–87. Harrisburg, PA: Trinity International, 1998.

Beyer, Bryan. *Encountering the Book of Isaiah: A Historical and Theological Survey.* Grand Rapids: Baker Academic, 2007.

Campbell, Joseph. *Thou Art That.* Novato, CA: New World Library, 1998.

Chisholm, Robert B. "The Christological Fulfillment of Isaiah's Servant Songs." *Bibliotheca Sacra* 163 (2006) 387–404.

Collins, John J. "The Son of Man and the Saints of the Most High in the Book of Daniel." *Journal of Biblical Literature* 93 (1974) 50–66.

———. *The Apocalyptic Imagination: An Introduction to Jewish Apocalyptic Literature.* Grand Rapids: Eerdmans, 1998.

Conzelmann, Hans. *The Theology of St. Luke.* 1st Fortress Press ed. Philadelphia: Fortress Press, 1982.

Crossan, John Dominic. *The Historical Jesus.* San Francisco: HarperCollins, 1991.

Davies, W. D., and Dale C. Allison. *The Gospel according to St. Matthew.* Vol. 3. Edinburgh: T. & T. Clark, 1997.

———. *A Critical and Exegetical Commentary on the Gospel according to Matthew.* Edinburgh: T. & T. Clark, 1997.

Derickson, Gary W. "Matthean Priority/Authorship and Evangelicalism's Boundary." *The Masters Seminary Journal* 14 (2003) 87–103.

Dodd, C. H. *History and the Gospel.* New York: Charles Scribner's Sons, 1938.

———. *The Parables of the Kingdom.* New York: Scribner, 1961.

Dunn, James D. G. "The Danielic Son of Man in the New Testament." In *Composition and Reception.* Vol. 2 of *The Book of Daniel*, edited by John

J. Collins and Peter W. Flint, 528–49. Betus Testamentum, Supplements 83.2. n.p.: Brill, 2001. https://doi.org/10.1163/9789004276093_012.

Eusebius. *The Ecclesiastical History of Eusebius Pamphilus, Bishop of Cesarea, in Palestine*. Translated by Christian Frederic Crusé. Philadelphia: R. Davis, 1833. https://catalog.hathitrust.org/Record/009722628.

Friedman, Theodore, and Harold Louis Ginsberg. "Isaiah." In *Encyclopaedia Judaica*, edited by Michael Berenbaum and Fred Skolnik, 10:57–75. Detroit: Macmillan Reference, 2007.

Friedrich, Gerhard, ed. *The Theological Dictionary of the New Testament*. Grand Rapids: Eerdmans, 1972.

Geldenhuys, Norval. *Commentary on the Gospel of St. Luke*. Grand Rapids: Eerdmans, 1979.

Ginsberg, Harold Louis. "The Book of Daniel." In *Encyclopedia Judaica*, edited by Michael Berenbaum and Fred Skolnik, 5:419–25. Detroit: Macmillan Reference, 2007.

Godet, Francis. *The Gospel of St. Luke*. New York: I. K. Funk & Co., 1881.

Graham, Ronald William. "C H Dodd and His Interpreters." *Lexington Theological Quarterly* 8 (1973) 1–10.

Hartman, Louis F., and Alexander A. Di Lella. *The Book of Daniel: A New Translation*. New York: Doubleday, 1983.

Hatina, Thomas. *Biblical Interpretation in the Early Christian Gospels: The Gospel of Luke*. London: T. & T. Clark, 2006.

Herbert, A. S. *The Book of the Prophet Isaiah 40–66*. Cambridge: Cambridge University Press, 1975.

Heskett, Randall. *Messianism within the Scriptural Scroll of Isaiah*. International Clark, 2007.

Janowski, Bernd. "He Bore Our Sins: Isaiah 53 and the Drama of Taking Another's Place." In *The Suffering Servant: Isaiah 53 in Jewish and Christian Sources*, edited by Peter Stuhlmacher, 48–75. Grand Rapids: Eerdmans, 2004.

Just, Arthur A. *Ancient Christian Commentary on Scripture: Luke*. Downers Grove, IL: InterVarsity, 2003.

Leske, Adrian M. "Jesus as a Nazarene." In *Resourcing New Testament Studies: Literary, Historical, and Theological Essays in Honor of David L. Dungan*, edited by Allan J. McNicol et al., 69–81. New York: Bloomsbury, 2011.

———. "Matthew." In *The International Bible Commentary: A Catholic and Ecumenical Commentary for the 21st Century*, edited by William R. Farmer, 1253–330. Collegeville, MN: Liturgical, 1998.

———. *The Prophetic Vision and the Real Jesus: Growth of the Prophetic Vision and Its Impact on the Mission of Jesus in Matthew's Gospel*. Eugene, OR: Wipf & Stock, 2017.

Lucas, Ernest. *Daniel*. Downers Grove: InterVarsity, 2002.

McKenzie, John L, trans. *Second Isaiah*. The Anchor Bible 20. Garden City, NY: Doubleday, 1968.

Mitchell, Christopher Wright. *Our Suffering Savior: Resources for Lent and Easter Preaching and Worship Based on Isaiah 52:13–53:12.* St. Louis: Concordia, 2003.

Moore, Arthur L. *The Parousia in the New Testament.* Leiden: E. J. Brill, 1966.

Most, William G. "Did St. Luke Imitate the Septuagint?" *Journal for the Study of the New Testament* 15 (1982) 30–41.

Motyer, Alec J. *Isaiah: An Introduction and Commentary.* Downers Grove: InterVarsity, 1999.

Muilenburg, James. "The Book of Isaiah: Chapters 40–66," in *The Interpreters Bible,* 5:381–419, 422–773. New York: Abingdon Press, 1952.

North, Christopher R. *The Suffering Servant in Deutero-Isaiah: An Historical and Critical Study.* London: Oxford University Press, 1948.

O'Rourke, John J. "Fulfillment Texts in Matthew." *Catholic Biblical Quarterly* 24 (1962) 394–403.

Redditt, Paul L. "The Community Behind the Book of Daniel." *Perspectives in Religious Studies* 36 (2009) 321–39.

Robertson, Archibald Thomas. *Commentary on the Gospel according to Matthew.* New York: Macmillan, 1911.

Silver, Daniel Jeremy. *A History of Judaism.* New York: Basic Books, 1974.

Steinmann, Andrew. *Daniel.* St. Louis: Concordia, 2008.

Sullivan, Clayton. *Rethinking Realized Eschatology.* Macon, GA: Mercer University Press, 1988.

Tannehill, Robert C. *Luke.* Abingdon New Testament Commentaries 3. Nashville: Abingdon Press, 1996.

———. *The Narrative Unity of Luke-Acts: A Literary Interpretation.* Philadelphia: Fortress, 1986.

Tharekadavil, Antony. *Servant of Yahweh in Second Isaiah.* Frankfurt: Peter Lang, 2007.

Ulrich, Daniel W. "The Missional Audience of the Gospel of Matthew." *Catholic Biblical Quarterly* 69 (2007) 64–83.

Viviano, B. T. "Kingdom of God." In *New Catholic Encyclopedia,* 8:172–75. New York: McGraw-Hill, 1996.

Webb, Barry G. *The Message of Isaiah.* Downers Grove: InterVarsity, 1996.

Wenham, David. "The Kingdom of God and Daniel." *Expository Times* 98.5 (1987) 132–34.

Westermann, Claus. *Isaiah 40–66: A Commentary.* Philadelphia: Westminster, 1969.

Wilken, Robert Louis, et al., eds. *Isaiah: Interpreted by Early Christian and Medieval Commentators.* The Church's Bible. Grand Rapids: Eerdmans, 2007.

Yarbro-Collins, Adela. "The Origin of the Designation of Jesus as 'Son of Man.'" *Harvard Theological Review* 10 (1987) 391–407.

Zevit, Ziony. "The Structure and Individual Elements of Daniel 7." *Zeitschrift für die Alttestamentliche Wissenschaft* 80 (1968) 385–96.

www.ingramcontent.com/pod-product-compliance
Lightning Source LLC
Chambersburg PA
CBHW060311100426
42812CB00003B/737